*The*

# ENCHANTED WILDERNESS

## *A Red Rock Odyssey*

## *By*

# *Ward J. Roylance*

D1207688

FOUR CORNERS WEST
Torrey, Utah 84775

TO THOSE
WHO CARE

Published by
  Four Corners West
  Box 117
  Torrey, Utah 84775

ISBN 0-915272-29-6

Photographs by the author unless otherwise attributed.

Front cover -
Waterpocket Fold: Domes of Capitol Reef

# CONTENTS

PROLOGUE                                                    5

THE INEFFABLE                                               9

Part One    THE AWAKENING                                  19

            Dead Horse Point              19
            Geocentric Stirrings         23
            Probings and Flounderings    29

Part Two    DISCOVERY: THE STATE                           69

            Foundations of a Career      69
            The Travel Council Era       73
            On My Own                    87

Part Three  ENLIGHTENMENT: THE ENCHANTED WILDERNESS        91

            Widening Horizons: The Colorado
              Plateau                    91
            Birth of a Concept           92
            School of the Earth          96
            The Enchanted Wilderness
              Association                101

Part Four   NEW BEGINNINGS: SLEEPING RAINBOW YEARS        103

            Torrey                      103
            Revelations in Geology      117

Part Five   THE VISION: A MILLENNIAL DREAM                125

            A State and An Image        126
            A Millennial Dream          136

Part Six    DIRECTION AND INDIRECTION                     145

            Desecration                 145
            Omens                       147
            Directions                  154

*A voice is in the wind I do not know;*
*A meaning on the face of the high hills*
*Whose utterance I cannot comprehend.* . . .
                    *MacDonald*

# PROLOGUE

**The Enchanted Wilderness** is the symbol name for a very special part of the earth. The name refers not only to the region's physical attributes but connotes its ineffable qualities as well.

That special place is a topographic province of the western United States known formally as the Colorado Plateau – or, by some geographers, as the Colorado Plateaus. In this book the province is referred to variously (and somewhat randomly) as the Enchanted Wilderness, the Colorado Plateau, the Plateau, and the red-rock country.

By whatever name it might be called, this great province is as distinctive in its own peculiar personality as, say, the Alps of Europe, the Amazon Basin of South America, the Sahara of Africa, the steppes or Himalayas of Asia. Actually, its natural characteristics could hardly differ more than they do from those regions – or, in fact, from most other topographic sections of the world.

The Colorado Plateau includes large parts of Arizona, Colorado, New Mexico and Utah. In size it approximates New Mexico, one of the larger states.

The province merits the name "plateau" both in a general and specific sense. Considered as a whole, it is a giant sedimentary platform that has been lifted several thousand feet above sea level. Into this platform or mother plateau, streams have gouged a labyrinth of steep-walled drainage channels, some of which – Grand Canyon and Desolation Canyon, for example – are as much as 5,000 feet deep. Mountainous uplifts, mesas, buttes, ridges and "standing rocks" – all in astonishing variety of size, shape and form – rise above the general level of the mother plateau to altitudes of 12,000 feet or more.

Because of factors such as characteristics of the region's rocks, climate and structural history, the majority of buttes and mesas, and a number of larger uplifts, display relatively flat summits or crests. Massive tabular highlands on the mother plateau (in Utah and Colorado particularly) are themselves called plateaus. Hence the name "Colorado Plateaus", a regional appellation preferred by some authorities.

The name "red-rock country" derives from the dominant color of the province. However, the mere word "red" creates a false impression, for the Plateau's reds are a world of color in themselves, ranging the gamut of hue, lightness and saturation on the color scale. Red, pink, orange and brown are categories of red most often noted, but those color-words are only grossly indicative of what is seen, since the region's reds are intricately combined with other colors, and those combinations intermixed with still others. The Indian term Sleeping Rainbow, applied to a particularly colorful rock group, could be applied with justification to the entire region.

Distinctive and unusual coloration, then, is a peculiarity of the Colorado Plateau. So, too, are uniqueness and variation of inorganic form. The Plateau consists of literally hundreds of different types of rocks, primarily of sedimentary origin but complemented by an assortment of igneous and metamorphic rocks. Since, for the most part, the Plateau is a high desert in the cyclic stage of disintegration, these rocks are being exposed and sculptured into shapes, forms and designs of limitless variation. No other part of the world even approaches the Plateau in this respect.

Resplendent colors and exotic forms, therefore, are distinguishing attributes of the Plateau. Viewed under conditions of everlasting transformation- the illusions of changing perspective and light - the Plateau is a magic land, an enchanted landscape if ever there could be such a thing.

Exotic colors and forms, and a special enchantment resulting therefrom: those qualities typify the Colorado Plateau. Add to them the wildness of the Plateau and the result is America's Enchanted Wilderness, for the Plateau is one of the least-developed, least-populated, least-known regions of the country.

Despite its remarkable concentration of national parks and monuments, state parks, national forests and recreation areas, and Indian reservations, the Plateau **as an integrated region** of natural wonders beyond comprehension is not known to the public at large. Not being known, it is not appreciated **as a region** and its destiny is of little concern to the general public. Its fate is being decided by uninspired officials, politicians and special interests, few of whom have an enlightened vision of **WHAT SHOULD. BE** and **WHAT MIGHT BE.**

This book is a love story that began more than forty years ago with my first journey to the red-rock country of southeastern Utah. The infatuation that saw its beginnings there at Dead Horse Point expanded to include the State of Utah. Eventually, joined in this infatuation by my dear companion Gloria, my love affair grew to embrace the entire Colorado Plateau - the marvelous Enchanted Wilderness - of the Four Corner states.

**A word of clarification:** Though I freely interchange the terms Enchanted Wilderness and Colorado Plateau to signify the same region, in my own mind there is emphasis on correlating the Enchanted Wilderness more specifically with the Canyonlands and High Plateaus divisions of the Plateau in Utah. I do this for several reasons:

(1) The Plateau's Indian lands in the four states are subject to different ownership and developmental influences, and will certainly have a different fate, than government lands which make up so much of the Plateau in Utah.

(2) Canyonlands and the High Plateaus of Utah are more remarkable, scenically and geologically-geographically, than other parts of the Plateau (with some notable exceptions); therefore, in my opinion, their developmental fate is of primary concern at this time.

(3) My personal experience has been heavily weighted in favor of Canyonlands and the High Plateaus of Utah.

Nevertheless, many points of argument made in this book respecting indiscriminate development apply as well to other parts of the Plateau.

*For we, which now*
   *behold . . .*
*Have eyes to wonder,*
   *but lack tongues to*
*praise.*

        Shakespeare

# THE INEFFABLE

*In Nature's infinite book of secrecy*
*A little I can read.*

Shakespeare

Indescribable or unspeakable: That is the ineffable.
The ineffable, by definition, is beyond expression.

What Gloria and I see from the heights of Thousand Lake
Mountain and the Aquarius Plateau is, to us, ineffable.
It is beyond expression, even comprehension. We look out
upon a convoluted jumble of practically every landscape
form imaginable - a library of earth history, a museum of
nature's surreal art.

There are cliffs and buttes, mountains and mesas, canyons and valleys, domes and pinnacles, rounded slopes and
numberless smaller forms, all painted in a rainbow spectrum of glorious hues, sculptured into shapes-designs-
patterns that astonish with strange and endless diversity.

We cannot possibly do justice to those vistas in written or spoken words. We cannot even verbalize them to
ourselves while looking. Language was not designed for
the articulation of mystic profundities, or the conveying
of emotional nuances, except in the vaguest way.

How could I describe, for instance, the overwhelming
impression of vastness and visual impact - the sensation
of being suspended as in a motionless plane, 4,000 feet
above the most sublime exhibit of rock esthetics either of
us has ever set eyes upon?

Or how could I describe those powerful feelings of
immemorial Time engendered by the ruins before us? The
inexorable cycles of change and decay these ruins manifest
- the inconceivable ages of creation and destruction they
represent? The hopelessness we feel about ever possessing

more than the merest fragment of knowledge about ancient
landscapes that preceded the ones we see: their myriad life
forms, the eons of their duration, the endless complexi-
ties of geological origins, causes and effects?

As we look out from Thousand Lake Mountain and the
Aquarius, impressions so ethereal they cannot be captured
in words glide fleetingly through our consciousness.
(Can those impressions even be termed thoughts?) They do
not require words, they defy words, and they could not be
conveyed with words.

Those impressions - those emotions - those convictions
of the soul - are *ineffable*.

". . . a riddle wrapped in a mystery inside an enigma,"
wrote Winston Churchill. He was speaking of the acts of
Russia and not the messages of nature, but his words describe, as succinctly as a few words can, how Gloria and
I regard the mysteries of the Enchanted Wilderness.

Do we differ from other people in this attitude of
reverential awe at nature's works in this land? Surely we
do in some respects if not in all. This is a hypnotic
place that casts a spell on those who are susceptible.
Responses are all a matter of personal, temperamental idio-
syncrasy. My emotional reactions and Gloria's are amazingly alike, being flavored by mysticism, resulting from
an intimate, long-time, broad-range relationship with the
Enchanted Wilderness not common to most people's experience.

Familiarity has not brought contempt or satiation in
our case. On the contrary, it has amplified our wonder
and strengthened our conviction that what we perceive here
in this magical land is only the slightest suggestion of
what lies beneath the physical facade, indistinct but not
quite hidden, waiting only for each individual to lift the
veil according to personal inclination or capability.

*I have seen the Enchanted Wilderness with multiple eyes:*
*I have seen it with the wondering eyes of youth,*
*and with older eyes that marvel still.*
*I have beheld it as a writer, struggling vainly*
*after words;*
*I have probed it with the camera's eye, seeking essence*
*that eludes.*
*I examine it as a student of earth and learn it has*
*no counterpart.*
*I view its mysteries with impassioned love and discover*
*sublimity.*
*I see it as a vision; it is before me as a dream.*
*Here I touch the ineffable grail.*

A mere listing of inspirational viewpoints in the Plateau region would fill pages. What is seen and felt from every one of them lies in the realm of the inexpressible. How do you verbalize Exaltation? Grandeur? The awesome? Eternity before your eyes? Adjectives fail. How do you even hint at the infinite nuances of inorganic art displayed here?

*Man's words do not serve well as conveyors of his deepest moods, his sacred thoughts and most-felt "inexpressibles".*
*Words are pale verbalizations of emotions that swell when faced with concepts too boundless to understand.*
*What can we do, for example, when confronted with Grand Canyon's cosmic truths?*
*Stand mute, perhaps (that's best), and muse about its nuances of time and immensity.*

And how do you articulate boundless Illusion wrought on forms of endless and exotic variety by shifting perspective, moving clouds, the amplifying or muting of light, shadings so mobile they change by the moment?

"Through forms we can explore a world closed to rational thought," said an ancient Egyptian.

What is Real in this bewitched landscape? Are there any natural Absolutes here that can be captured and solidified by the living eye? (By the camera, perhaps, which records a mere moment.) For the thinking person, illusion-reality-absolutes are of more than casual concern in this enchanted land.

We look, Gloria and I. We study and analyze. We photograph. We visit and revisit. No place is ever the same. We see a form or design; in a moment it has changed. As Gloria says:

*The Enchanted Wilderness:*
*A mysterious, changing place;*
*Never the same,*
*Tricking our thoughts, touching our inner beings,*
*Probing our deeper minds;*
*Giving rise to philosophical whisperings,*
*Conveying elusive truths that point*
*To the Ineffable.*

In Torrey our south windows look out over a sweeping expanse of fields, toward a horizon formed by the Aquarius Plateau. Great buttress slopes, dark and somber, flow down

The Cockscomb and Aquarius Plateau (Boulder Mountain)
from our windows.

from precipices ringing the mountain's table crest.

Low mesas and Cockscomb ridge provide middleground accent and perspective.  The Cockscomb is a jagged exposure of light-colored Navajo sandstone, upthrust and fractured in some remote age by the Teasdale fault.  Though not too remarkable either structurally or esthetically in this region of surpassing earth forms, it is a prominent land-mark.  When we glimpse it from Fish Lake Pass, 25 miles away, we know we are nearly home.

The Cockscomb is meaningful to us as a symbol.  It represents immutable reality and permanence on the one hand, unreality and illusion on the other.  In miniature it typifies those qualities as they are found throughout the Plateau region.

Several years ago I began photographing the Cockscomb at different times of day and seasons of the year, under varied weather and lighting conditions.  Eventually I com-pared 20 or 30 of those photos.  The results were fasci-nating.  Every picture showed a radically different Cocks-comb!  Which was the "real" Cockscomb?  All were real, of course; and all were illusions in the sense that they never appeared the same.

Viewing from any fixed point affords only a tantaliz-ing intimation of all the mystical qualities of this strange land.  Awesome and inspiring as they may be, land-scapes seen in overview are only grand mosaics - or they might be likened to the collective exhibits of a great museum of art as seen from a distance.  The encompassing whole is marvelous; separate elements of the grand dis-play, however, are indistinct.  In the Enchanted Wilder-ness, as in a museum or with a great mural, stand-back viewing should be accompanied by close inspection for ulti-mate appreciation.

Most first time visitors to this region are overwhelmed by the landscape as a whole and by its larger, more strik-ing features.  There is far too much to assimilate at one time.  Repeat visits are required - sometimes many visits - before one becomes gradually aware of myriad smaller, more intricate, less obtrusive details that tend to elude the unpracticed eye.

I speak from long years of experience.  My argument is supported by thousands of scenic photos which reveal def-inite change (I like to think of it as positive evolution) in my choice of subject matter.  For 20 or 30 years I was so preoccupied with macrocosmic esthetics and marvels of

earth structure that I hardly glanced at the smaller but
more exquisite rock art that abounds throughout the red-
rock country: marvelous reliefs, or free-standing, exotic
mini-sculptures, or rock textures so beautiful they bring
tears to the eyes.

These small-scale works of natural art have not replaced
the landscape in our affections. Rather, they expand our
world of appreciation enormously.

Near Torrey, for example, is an expanse of chocolate-
colored, multi-layered sedimentary rock known as the Moenkopi formation. The area is extremely rugged, a fact not
too apparent from a distance. It is, in truth, a labyrinth
of steep-walled canyons, shallow in their upper ends,
dropping off rapidly in sharp ledges to gorges that are
hundreds of feet deep. Here is the epitome of ruin. Broken
sandstone is everywhere, but those rocks create a fairyland
of erosional artistry beyond description.

Gloria and I have spent hundreds of hours in that weird
land, hiking along the shattered rims and ledges, marveling at the wonderful designs that never exhaust the possibilities of surface and profile sculpturing. Worlds of
art are here, worlds never dreamed by human mind, fantasies
created from molecules by water and wind.

Some of those designs – many of them – make us cringe
with delight. They are so *beautiful*! Seemingly so *purposeful*! They defy description. Or, more accurately, what
defies description – what is inexpressible – is the **idea
of esthetic perfection** behind the visible symbols cut into
the rock. For many of these designs are esthetically perfect, insofar as we are qualified to judge: perfect in
form, balance, and harmonious relationship between individual elements. Their spontaneous originality is breathtaking.

Whereas organic designs, and those created by people,
tend to be stereotyped in cases, or formally geometric, or
repetitious and stylized, every design carved in rock is
an original. In inorganic art there seems to be no dupli-
cation or repetition. Line flow and form, in rock, have
limitless variations in three dimensions.

Esthetic perfection in nature, as a concept, is hardly
novel. Most people recognize it in flowers, sunsets,
mountains, the forms of animal life, etc. So it is not
surprising that rock forms also can provide the inspiration of "felt" perfection: for example, the gigantic
"temples" of Zion and Capitol Reef...the rock forests of

Bryce Canyon...the natural arches of Arches National Park and the Escalante...the spires and flowing rock of The Needles-Salt Creek country.

I have always found esthetic pleasure in rock art of that type, and not only in form and texture. Colors of the rocks in the Enchanted Wilderness are so marvelous, as at Bryce, or Cedar Breaks, or Capitol Reef, or in The Needles-Salt Creek country, or myriad other places.

Trying to describe erosional forms is very difficult for me. Particularly difficult to describe are intricately detailed sculptures, such as those at Bryce and Cathedral Valley, which are carved from layered rocks of varying thickness and differing resistance to erosion. In my personal lexicon, such forms represent the ineffable.

So, too, do some of the great dome-buttes of Zion and Capitol Reef and the San Rafael Swell. I am not capable of imagining designs more emotionally satisfying than those which nature has provided in the red-rock country (speaking here of inorganic designs). Oh, some purposeful touching-up and rounding-off of rough edges might be beneficial, but no major restructuring would be required to satisfy my esthetic standards.

On the subject of arches: Since we have begun focussing from the large to the small, Gloria and I have discovered a fantastic microcosmic world of "openings" that surpass in complexity of design their larger counterparts.

Even Delicate and Grosvenor arches - artistic masterpieces as they are - cannot compare in this way with literally countless small carvings on rock faces of the Enchanted Wilderness. These miniature creations display every conceivable variation of arch and window forms, combined with exquisite pillars, domes, alcoves, grottoes, pilasters and other architectural elements.

This type of mini-sculpturing occurs in many of the Plateau's rock layers, particularly on canyon walls where water has flowed at one time or another. Rock surfaces of the Capitol Reef area, for example, display countless exhibits of that nature; also North Wash between Hanksville and Lake Powell ...the Circle Cliffs...Factory Bench. The list of sites could be lengthened indefinitely. We have personal knowledge of only a few.

Gloria and I are intrigued at the moment by rock-surface designs of the San Rafael and Morrison rock groups, which include the Carmel, Entrada, Curtis, Summerville, Salt Wash and Brushy Basin sandstones, mudstones and shales.

Being relatively youthful, these rocks are fairly soft.
They erode easily, and they have been carved into an astonishing variety of shapes and textures ranging from very
small to very large.

For example, the giant temple-buttes of Cathedral Valley
and South Desert are products of those rocks, or several
of them in combination. So are the many miles of sculptured
cliff faces in that region. Those cliff faces, and the
buttes themselves, flaunt an endlessly variegated display
of relief and freestanding carvings that leave one speech-
less with admiration. If any exhibit of rock esthetics
can be termed "ineffable", this region's can.

I could go on, listing and describing points and places
in the Enchanted Wilderness that display natural artistry
approaching what Gloria and I consider the esthetic ideal.

An important point I have tried to make here is that
there is artistry in the Plateau region sufficient to satisfy anybody with artistic sensitivity - if not of this
generation, then surely in future years.

The more one looks, the more (magically) there is to see.
There can be no end to esthetic discovery in this land,
because artistic stimuli are as omnipresent here as they
are likely to be anywhere, with respect at least to
inorganic art. The landscape here is one of idealized,
archetypal forms: an intricate natural mosaic of surprise,
expectation, anticipation, and excitement.

In sum: Unbelievably rich, inexhaustible **diversity**
of form and design is one of the wonders of the Enchanted
Wilderness. So, too, is the **uniqueness** or uncommonness
of so many of these forms and designs. And the miracle of
how they are **perceived** in forever-changing, never-the-same
aspects, which vary according to time of day, conditions
of the sky, seasons and weather. Not least, how marvelous is the dimensional **range** of natural phenomena from
panoramic landscapes to exquisite rock designs of microcosmic size.

Emotions overflow when I attempt, so feebly, to describe
the Plateau as I know and feel it. After 40-odd years it
is more wonderful to me than ever. Gloria and I cannot
comprehend it, and know we never will. It conveys its
multiple messages in complex cryptography, decipherable
only by those who know the codes. Some of those codes we
have mastered. Other people have succeeded where we have
failed. But there are inexpressible messages yet waiting
to be read. Of that we are convinced.

## Part One

# THE AWAKENING

*If Utah's mountains are its inspiration,*
*the incomparable red-rock country is its*
*pride and joy. Here is something unique*
*- something unequalled anywhere else on*
*earth.*

Utah Trails Vol. 2

### DEAD HORSE POINT

Once sparked, the infatuation developed quickly. Even
before setting foot in the red-rock country, I knew I
must see it.

The year was 1942 and I was 21. Pearl Harbor was a
recent memory, the United States was at war and millions of young men awaited induction. I was one of them.
Having a few weeks of free time between my resignation
from my job in Salt Lake City and the date for voluntary
induction, I had planned a trip to the red-rock country
of southeastern Utah.

What influence the printed word can have! In 1941
the Federal Writers Project published *Utah: A Guide to
the State*, and I had purchased one of the first copies.
The book fascinated me. I was entranced by its descriptions of southern and southeastern Utah, that little
known region of red rocks, bottomless gorges, and erosional forms that seem not to belong to this world.

"US 160 runs through a country in which shades of red
permeate almost everything - plains, deserts, hills,
cliffs, canyons," said the guidebook. How extraordinary
such a land must be, I thought. I had never seen that
country, nor had I read about it except in the novels of
Zane Grey. Yet it called to me from the pages of that
Utah guidebook.

Arches National Monument ... Natural Bridges
National Monument ... Rainbow Bridge ... Monument

Valley ... the LaSal Mountains ... the Old Spanish
Trail ... Major Powell and the Colorado-Green ...
wildness and romance, exploration and discovery.

Most intriguing to me was the book's description of
Dead Horse Point. "The trail crosses the neck, a narrow
strip of land separating two yawning gorges each more than
a thousand feet deep. These gorges dwindle into insignif-
icance when the trail comes to a dizzy, teetering halt at
the rim of the UPPER GRAND CANYON OF THE COLORADO. Here
the face of the earth breaks away into a 3,000-foot chasm,
offering perhaps the most sensational canyon panorama in
Utah...."

In my case those words were an irresistible invitation.
I succeeded in enticing two of my younger brothers,
Byron and Bill, and a young cousin to accompany me on the
great adventure.

Our vehicle was my little convertible roadster with
rumble seat, a Ford V-8 of 1932 vintage. Intervening
years had brought modifications of diverse and drastic
nature, and by 1942 it was not a trustworthy conveyance.
Nevertheless, it was all we had, and considering the
abominable sideroads it was forced to endure, our little

The author, southeastern Utah 1942.

conveyance performed well.  We dropped the muffler and
gas cap (later recovered), the springs required several
realignments, and the engine gulped a quart of oil every
30 miles.  Other than those inconveniences, as well as
swarms of gnats, heat, sunburn, and lack of water, we
had an enjoyable five days.

Dead Horse Point was our first night's stop.  While
the others drove back along the road in search of water, I
sat on the edge of the Orange Cliffs precipice, trying to
comprehend and emotionally digest the tumultous sea of
bare rock that began 2,000 vertical feet below the eyrie
on which I perched and rolled away in chaotic convolutions
toward mystic horizons.

Dropping into dusk, the late afternoon sun was engaged
in that indescribable interplay of light and shadow that
always transforms the corrugations of Canyonlands - its
mesas, buttes, escarpments, gorges, mountain peaks, and
infinitude of smaller forms - into a fantasy of unearthly
designs and shapes.

Never before had I experienced such a visual phantasma-
goria, or such **silence**.  That complete absence of sound
overwhelmed, oppressed, even frightened me.  Except for

The Enchanted Wilderness from Dead Horse Point.

the flitting gnats there was no visible movement in the
universe around me. The air was still, the river too far
away for detection of water flow. Time had stopped and
I was suspended between earth and sky.

On that same trip we visited a section of the Arches
and two of the three White Canyon bridges. Roads were
terribly rough; it would be many years before they were
paved. My journal entry for June 9 was written at a table
at the end of the road near Edwin Bridge in Natural Bridges
National Monument. "It's now 9:20 and we're all plenty
tired.... We had a hell of a time over that awful road
here from Blanding. It took us 3½ hours and the front
springs got out of place again."

Before leaving next day I perused the old register, a
priceless document containing dates and names as far back
as 1925. Many were known to me even at that time:
Harold Bell Wright (1925) ... Herbert Gregory (geologist)
... George H. Dern and Henry H. Blood (Utah governors) ...
Sylvester Q. Cannon, Bryant S. Hinckley, Albert E. Bowen,
Oscar McConkie (Mormon Church authorities) ... Wallace F.
Bennett (businessman and senator) ... Dr. F. J. Pack
(geologist) ... explorers Norman D. Nevills, Harry Goulding and Emery C. Kolb. One person registered from Bel-
gium, one from Germany, and several from England.

We hiked to Sipapu (Augusta) Bridge. "I'm afraid we
don't appreciate this country," I wrote later. Nothing
compared then, or afterwards for many years, with the
emotional impact of the view from Dead Horse Point. "It
spoiled everything else - for me, anyway," I wrote at
the time. I found it superlative and sublime. It remains
so now, in deep recesses where I recall it as it was and
not as it has been since industrial mutilation.

I perceive that first experience at Dead Horse Point as
a mystical enlightenment. It determined the main directions of my life's work, though there were to be so many
diversions along the way that only from late-life perspective can I see its significance.

Dead Horse Point, for nearly 30 years, epitomized the
red-rock country for me. I considered it the grandest
sight this side of heaven. I returned to it time and time
again. Primarily its appeal was an emotional one, dependent less on my actual presence atop the teetering rim of
the Orange Cliffs than on the meanings deep inside me:
of Space, represented by the vastness of skyscape and
landscape that began literally at the rim ... of limitless
Time, suggested graphically by the ruins of rock that I

knew were the products of incomprehensible eons of building
up and tearing down ... of vivid, vibrant colors and combinations of colors ... of strange forms and designs and
their intricate relationships. Though I saw the landscape
with my eyes, I **felt** it more vividly with my soul.

> *There is no excellent beauty that*
> *hath not some strangeness in*
> *the proportion.*

### Francis Bacon

Even today, when I think of Dead Horse Point, there are
emotional stirrings resulting from overwhelming dimension.
But there is the remembrance, also, of primeval wildness.
For nearly 30 years after my first visit, that land showed
few signs of mutilation by mankind. It was virgin! Boats
had plied the river but left no enduring mark. Oil drill
probings could not be seen from the rim. Livestock left
few apparent marks. Dirt roads, such as they were, seemed
not as obtrusive then as now.

This emotional residue is why I have rarely visited
Dead Horse Point since 1971, when a potash mining company
mutilated the landscape with huge evaporation ponds in
full view below the rim. The hurt is still too painful.
So is the lingering bitterness toward officials and news
media who helped to bring this travesty about, and kept
its visual impacts from public knowledge until the ponds
were built. Not that I believe, even now, that enough
people would have objected if they had known in advance
of what was planned. Americans in general, and Utahns in
particular, were not easily aroused enmasse - in those
days - in opposition to such developments in pristine wilderness.

## GEOCENTRIC STIRRINGS

I am not a native Utahn. My parents, however, were
born in Utah and all my ancestors arrived in Utah within
the first decade of settlement. My father's family were
early settlers of Springville in Utah Valley, some of
them becoming prominent there in various fields. Members
of my mother's family colonized Cache Valley in 1860,
the Uinta Basin in 1879, and the Snake River Valley of
eastern Idaho in the 1890s. My parents met and were
married in Idaho, soon moved to Oregon (where I was born)

and returned to Idaho for a few years.  In 1929 our family migrated to Los Angeles, returning to Salt Lake City
the following year when I was not quite ten years of age.
Ever since, except for interludes of travel and brief
residence in other places, Utah has been my home.

The years of my youth in Salt Lake City, prior to the
Dead Horse Point trip in 1942, introduced me to the mountains, valleys and deserts of northern and central Utah.
Infatuation with Utah was born during my teens, though I
did not then recognize it as such.  Perhaps it first mani-
fested in elementary school when I compiled a scrapbook
on Utah for one of my classes.

Our family was very poor in a material way, as were
the majority of people during the Great Depression years
of the 1930s.  There were six of us children, five boys
and one girl:  Duane, myself, Darrell, Byron, Bill and
Phyllis, the youngest.  We older boys did what we could
to supplement the family larder and income.  We picked up
coal along the railroad tracks and went from door to
door, selling such things as homemade glue and towels
made by my mother from flour sacks.

Even before our teens, Duane and I were avid readers.
We haunted Chapman Branch Library, a mile from home.
Mother encouraged this interest in books.  We both read
all the Tarzan titles we could find, and Zane Grey, and
Rider Haggard's exciting novels.  I loved tales of adventure and exploration.  Romantic history fascinated me.
The movie "Lost Horizons", with its fabled Shangri-la,
amplified a deep fascination with the Himalayas that
began in Fourth Grade geography.  Half a century elapsed
before I was to see them in person and be transformed in
the process.

Many times we boys would hitchhike or walk to and from
Bountiful, Centerville, and Farmington, 10 to 14 miles
away.  There we picked orchard fruits and berries, usually
for less than a dollar a day.  Now and then we would
journey 30 miles south to Alpine in Utah Valley, where my
mother's cousin Evelyn and her husband, "Uncle Will",
supported their two girls and two boys with a small farm,
orchard, and chickens.  They were generous with us, loading us up with apples, raspberries, milk, potatoes and
other food.

Alpine during the 1930s was a rustic, old-fashioned
village, most of its people depending for a precarious
livelihood on chicken-raising, dairying, fruit-growing
and gardening.  Since then it has become a colony of sorts

for artists and others who have fallen under the spell of the giant Wasatch peaks that ring it on two sides and inspire its name.

My youthful days in Alpine – most of them happy or content – helped to develop a deep and lasting affection for Utah Valley, its stupendous mountains and shining lake. I was beguiled especially by American Fork Canyon, which yawned close by, and the soaring white slopes of the Lone Peak-Pfeiferhorn massif to the north. In those days, before Geneva Steel Works and the auto pollution of more recent times, the air of Utah Valley was relatively clean and the mountains could be seen in their glory much more often than now. In one of those youthful years I climbed to the top of Mount Timpanogos, joining hundreds of others who made that pilgrimage. A popular annual affair for many years, the climb was eventually discontinued because of ecological damage.

Darrell and I spent several summers in Indianola, near Fairview in central Utah, helping our Houtz cousins with their haying. Being city boys, I doubt that we even earned our keep, but Aunt Ethel (my father's aunt), Uncle Gus, Buddy and LaMar were kind to us. They had no money to pay us, but their table overflowed with good food. They fed

Peaks of the Wasatch Mountains from Utah Valley.

us when food was scarce at home, and their open-hearted hospitality lured us back to Indianola many times over the years - for rabbit hunting, deer hunting, and just visiting with people we loved. Though I abandoned hunting and fishing at an early age, and soon learned I would never be a rancher, isolated little Indianola in its mountain valley fostered my growing infatuation with Utah's vast spaces.

During the early 1930s, when I was 12 or 13, our Mormon ward sponsored Fathers' and Sons' outings. I suppose such events also were sponsored by other wards in the valley. Whatever the case, our ward transported fathers and their sons up Big Cottonwood Canyon to The Spruces, a community campground, where they camped several days and nights in an alpine setting near Brighton Resort.

Though my own father never accompanied us on those outings, I will carry to my grave those memories - engraved on soul - of the grandeur of the cupping peaks, the fragrance of evergreens, the cosmic sound of water pouring swiftly-hynotically-endlessly downhill. It was there, in that most magnificent of Utah's mountain gorges, that I first became truly aware of nature: of the star-filled sky, the earth and its majesty, the exuberance of native plants, and water with its mystic symbolisms. Or I believe it was there that the first whispered awareness of nature's manifestations came to me.

Also in those teen-years, as a Boy Scout, I joined my troop on two of its expeditions to Camp Steiner in the Uinta Mountains, not far from Mirror Lake. Camp Steiner is about 70 miles east of Salt Lake City in a densely-forested basin between high, bare, rocky peaks. The camp is on the shore of Scout Lake, and I suppose the scouts who still go there today - 50 years after my own visits - experience what we experienced then. That is, except for the road. In those days it was not paved east of Kamas, so we bounced and jounced atop our duffel in a dusty open truck for 30 or 40 miles each way. Being young and happy, we didn't mind too much.

Scout Lake and Mirror Lake are in a region of glacial lakes, at or near the headwaters of the Weber, Provo, Bear and Duchesne rivers. The lake basin itself is high, at 10,000 feet, and timberline begins not far above its floor. Three great peaks dominate the scene in the vicinity of the lakes: Bald Mountain, Hayden Peak, and Mount Agassiz, all about 12,000 feet or more in altitude.

Others, higher and lower, stretch away to west and east.
It has always stirred me to think of that primeval Uinta
wilderness with its myriad lakes and ponds, hundreds of
miles of trails to be explored, and skyscraping summits to
be climbed.

Those were magic youthful days at Scout Lake. Most
details were long ago lost to memory, but I still recall –
or feel with emotion – the crispness of the air and ici-
ness of the water. The campfires where we huddled in
warm companionship, listening to ghost stories, entranced
by the coals, the flames, the stars, the overwhelming
silence and mystery that filled the universe beyond our
little circle of light and life.

There was rafting, and daytime meanderings through
flowered meadows and groves of arrow-straight pines.
There were chipmunks to watch and feed; darting squirrels;
fish and birds. Most nostalgic of all is the remembrance
of **smell**: of cool fresh water, of campfire smoke, of
frying bacon and eggs, of outdoor toilets, of pine gum and
evergreen needles. Even the night air, cold and damp,
I remember more as a smell than a tactile sensation.

And there was the human element. As most young people
do, I yearned for peer companionship outside the family.

Hayden Peak and Mirror Lake Basin, Uinta Mountains.

Association in rustic, isolated settings such as that at Scout Lake brings people together, if not always on deep levels. That special communion hardly lasted beyond the days we spent at the lake, but it was precious at the time.

In the years since then I have returned to the Uintas many times. Not having been blessed with legs that allowed more than moderate walking, I have never penetrated the range's recesses on foot, other than climbing to the top of Bald Mountain, hiking to lakes such as Red Castle and to the headwaters of Yellowstone River. But I have flown over much of the range and have seen what is visible from roads on its periphery.

In my youth the Uinta peaks enthralled me with their lonely grandeur. It has always been obvious to me that they are not as dramatically rugged as those of the high Wasatch, but they are loftier, more remote, more inaccessible. That always made an emotional difference.

I understand why Edmund Hillary, first conqueror of Mount Everest, tried to be kind by terming them the "Friendly Mountains". And they are gentle mountains in respects. Compared with the Himalayas - and even the Alps, the Cascades, the Sierra Nevadas, the northern Rockies - that is what they are. Yet they have a majestic beauty and wild allure that set them apart. They need no apologetic defense.

There were other youthful probings in northern Utah prior to my first red-rock experience in 1942. My brothers and I always managed to have a car in the family, however old and decrepit it might be. We put our cars to use, testing them in all the nearby canyons. We made numerous trips to Jackson Hole, Yellowstone Park, and we often visited relatives in the Snake River Valley of Idaho. Parker, near St. Anthony, was our childhood home. Beloved uncles, aunts and cousins lived there; we visited them often. We drove to Lagoon and Saltair for dances, and foolishly taunted the treacherous flats east of Great Salt Lake. We hunted rabbits near Grantsville and in Skull Valley. There were many other exploratory excursions as well.

Northern Utah, therefore, or much of it, was known to me before my 21st birthday. Southern Utah, on the other hand, was a void insofar as first-hand knowledge was concerned. I was not aware of such a void, of course, being ignorant of that part of the world. There was not a spark of interest before I read those intriguing descriptions of the red-rock country in *Utah: A Guide to the State* in 1941.

That book marked my awakening to what Gloria and I later termed the **Enchanted Wilderness**. Awareness developed by degrees over time, and the name itself came nearly 30 years later. I am still discovering that mystic land with Gloria.

In the pages that follow I endeavor to show that there never can be an end to that process of discovery, for me or anybody else, who seriously explores the red-rock country.

## PROBINGS AND FLOUNDERINGS

The four years following our Dead Horse Point trip brought no opportunities for exploration in the red-rock country. The Army took me on assignments in California, Oregon, Maryland, Mississippi and to Europe, where I served in France, Germany and Austria. That travel opened my young-man's eyes to other places and peoples, at an age when I was old enough to observe and reflect upon sometimes traumatic experiences with a degree of maturity.

Those experiences of the outside world did nothing to lessen my longing for home - for family, friends and familiar scenes. I loved Salt Lake Valley and the Wasatch peaks. Even the Bavarian Alps and the stately volcanoes of Oregon and northern California failed to displace Utah's mountains in my affections. I passed through the lush landscapes of eastern America and Europe. Still I longed for the austere semideserts and mountains of Utah.

I was homesick then, and have been since, when away from Utah. No longer to such a painful extent, however, for the Wasatch Front has become so congested, polluted and "developed" that it does not resemble what I knew even 20 or 30 years ago. Now it is difficult for me to love that place. And family ties have loosened with the departure of older friends and relatives. Such changes make a difference in nostalgia. Also, Gloria and I have not lived in Salt Lake City since 1976. Our bodies, if not all of our hearts, reside primarily in the red-rock country, which now signifies Utah to us.

As a soldier, away from home, I worried about my future. I disliked accounting and stenography, for which I had trained. Medicine, architecture and engineering were favored possibilities, and I investigated them before

deciding I was too old or had not the talent. I floundered. But there was no urgency in making a decision.
The GI Bill promised at least four years of college.

The Army years enlightened me in ways other than just
travel and association with people of varied backgrounds.
I read a great deal. Free time hung heavy on my hands
and I spent much of it in the base libraries. My horizons
expanded as they never would at home. In Europe our
division traveled 800 miles through France, Germany and
Austria before the war ended in 1945. That was the rich-
est experential period of my youthful life. Being a
naive boy from the provinces, I had known little about
the outside world, or other cultures, or behavioral
values that differed from those of my own culture. So
I learned a great deal.

Since then I have traveled whenever circumstances
allowed, comparing Utah goegraphically and culturally
with other places. I believe this has not been done in
a negative way. Comparison is necessary for evaluative
growth.

Without the perspective of such travel, my enthusiasm
for Utah and the red-rock country would simply be a mani-
festation of ignorant and exaggerated geocentrism. It may,
in fact, be geocentrism, and perhaps it is exaggerated as
well. However, I do base that enthusiasm (qualified in
respects in later years) on experience that provides a
basis for comparison with other parts of the world.

. . . But I digress. There was much idle time on my
hands after VE Day, during the summer of 1945. Our outfit
was stationed at Enns, Austria, near Linz. Most of us
were unsure of the future. Old-timers could look forward
to stateside rotation or discharge, but those of us with
fewer service points resigned ourselves to Far East ship-
ment. At least we had a glimmer of hope that the war
might end eventually, perhaps soon. Our thoughts were
often of home and what we would do with our future lives.
Letters I wrote that summer to my brothers and mother preserved my thoughts about the red-rock country and how I
hoped to make it the basis for a career. In a letter to
Darrell, I wrote the following:

"After all the switching around, transferring from one
company and one job and one town to another all the time,
and all the traveling, I'm being ruined for a steady job.
Makes me sick to think of ever having to take another
dreary office job when I get out of the Army. I'll have

a thousand bucks or so (same as you) when I get out, and
I would still like to go into the sightseeing business.

"Did I ever tell you how I figure? Do you remember
the trip Byron, Bill, Kenny and I took a couple of years
ago down into the desert country? The one you didn't
care to go on? Well, hardly anyone has ever been down
there but there is really more to see than anywhere else
in the state. Slowly but surely people will learn about
that section and want to go there on trips. That's where
I'd like to come in.

"On a 'roughing-it' trip like it would have to be
(lack of improvements, bad roads, no towns, etc.), if just
a couple of people went in their own car they'd have more
trouble than enjoyment; they'd ruin their car on the bad
roads, probably get lost, run out of water or gas, and so
on. So I think a group of maybe 8 or 10, going together
in a special bus with a guide and all the equipment, food,
provisions, provided would solve the situation. 10 people
at $15.00 per day for 7 days ain't hay.

"You'll probably laugh at my idea as fanciful, and I
don't doubt much that it is, but at least it's something
to look forward to and think about.... Boy, that country
gets in your blood and you can't get it out. It's so
vast, so deserted, so unexplored, so desolate, and so
fascinating. Read about it in that Utah book if you
haven't sent it off already."

That dream never was realized to the extent I dreamed
it. And, as time went on, similar dreams of sightseeing
businesses in the red-rock country were turned into
reality by other people. Few succeeded on even a moderate scale. Some lost all they had invested.

But I didn't know that, of course; it was in the
future. The impracticality of my dreams did not become
apparent at once. I was still attempting various adapta-
tions 25 years later, and even now I think I would like
to make a living by introducing other people to the red-
rock country.

Apparently that is not to be, insofar as introducing
them **physically** to the region is concerned. I now realize
that the Enchanted Wilderness is not just a place. It is
also, and more importantly, an **IDEA** beyond the senses.
Physical presence is not even required: witness my own conversion through the printed word, before I had even seen
the country. And physical presence does not guarantee a
revelation. Far from it. Of the millions who visit the

Enchanted Wilderness each year, only a few thousand -
probably even fewer than that - are animated by the **Idea**
behind the diversionary physical facade. More about that
later.

I was discharged from the Army in February 1946.
Within two weeks I was making inquiries of people in the
tour business as to the feasibility of my tour proposal.
Though mixed, the response did not discourage me from
placing an ad in an outdoor sports magazine. I learned
(oh, my naivete!) how difficult it was to obtain capital
for a fledgling, untried business. I was confused, un-
settled. I wrote, "Geez, this tour idea is driving me
batty. One minute I want to give it up as hopeless -
the next I'm enthused about it. But I keep getting
deeper all the time."

Circumstances finally defeated me. Responses to the
ad were inquiries only. When informed of what to expect
in the way of discomfort and inconvenience, the inquirers
lost their interest. By then I was enrolled at University
of Utah and had no resources or energy to invest in a
business. I abandoned the project but not the dream.

On a weekend in May 1946, almost exactly four years
after our first visit to the red-rock country, my brother
Bill and I attempted a return. We were accompanied by my
sister Phyllis, her girl friend, and my cousin Garth. We
traveled in our old 1939 Packard sedan, a faithless
behemoth that always repaid our abuse in kind, with interest.

Near Woodside we "ran into a snow storm and our wipers
wouldn't work. Then our generator stopped working. Got
six miles on the Dead Horse Point road and then turned
back because the road was wet and slippery as heck, and I
didn't know how good the battery was. So we went down
to Moab where I had a mechanic work on the generator for
two hours, without success. It's completely shorted out.
Gave him $2, then headed up to the Arches, Devils Garden
Section via Salt Valley Road. We parked for the night in
Salt Valley, about 15 miles from the highway."

The girls slept warmly in the car; the rest of us froze
outside. After breakfast, while the girls sunned themselves, we fellows hiked the broken ridge to the east "to
see if we could find the Devils Garden." We were in it
but didn't recognize it. After four hours we hadn't seen
an arch, but "we did see some huge fins, canyons, etc.
It's fascinating country." Back at the car we rested a
while, being very tired, then wired up the muffler, packed,

"pushed the car to start it (the starter wouldn't even connect) - and off for home." That haven was reached before dark, fortunately, because we had no lights.

"A nice time," I wrote. "Now the desert country is in my blood more than ever. Tourists will flock there some day."

That trip was more or less typical of uncounted other red-rock probings in future years. Always, it seems in retrospect, we encountered mechanical troubles, sand or mud, heat, cold, dust, rain, snow. We always had too little time. Distance from Salt Lake City was too great (200 to 300 miles each way). More often than not we were thwarted from reaching our planned goal.

Those difficulties only amplified the fascination for me. The call of the unknown red-rock wilds persisted. I never have been able to resist that call for long, and when the summons is answered it only tantalizes, never fully satisfies.

That summer of 1946 saw other trips. "Southern Utah is in my blood again," I wrote in June. Later that month, in the old Packard, Bill and I spent five days in the red-rock country. July brought trips to the Uintas and the Wasatch. In August we visited Bryce Canyon, Zion Canyon and Cedar Breaks. Over the Labor Day weekend several of us drove into the San Rafael Swell for the first time and reached Dead Horse Point for the second time.

Those red-rock excursions of that summer of 1946 - first-time visits for the most part - only increased my excitement.

Much of Utah's red-rock country in the 1940s was still relatively wild, but not completely so. Stockmen and prospectors had ranged most of it. Geologists had studied and written about much of it. It was mapped, if superficially. Some parks and monuments had been established. There were paved and (mostly) unpaved roads, though not yet the network of uranium roads, built by the Atomic Energy Commission during the 1950s, which were instrumental in opening up many formerly remote places in Canyonlands to motorized vehicles.

And yet only a few hundred people lived in the thousands of square miles between Price-Green River on the north and the Arizona border on the south, Highway 89 on the west and Moab-Monticello-Blanding on the east. This vast wilderness or near-wilderness is one of the most rugged regions on the planet, in a peculiar sense of ruggedness applicable mainly to intricately dissected sedimentary strata. It is a labyrinth of steep-walled canyons, washes, escarpments, mesas, buttes, plateaus, mountains - all in great variety of dimension, conformation, degree of slope, color, and rock composition. Superimposed on larger rock forms and surfaces is a literal infinitude of strange, exotic, unfamiliar designs and shapes, in relief or full dimensional form.

This wildness, ruggedness, strangeness, and infinite variety of form, design and color intrigued me from the beginning, though I have never been able satisfactorily to analyze or articulate their attraction. I am certain that physical attributes alone have not been responsible for the mystical effect of the red-rock country on me.

More important than the **actual** seeing of some wondrous scene or form or design has been the **anticipation** of suddently being rewarded by some new and unexpected attraction. It has been the exciting expectation of new discovery, as well as actual discovery itself, that has lured me back on hundreds of excursions over more than 40 years. Rarely if ever have I been disappointed in that respect.

What is it that confers the noblest delight?
What is that which swells a man's breast with pride
above that which any other experience can bring to
him? Discovery! To know that you are walking
where none others have walked, that you are behold-
ing what human eye has not seen before, that you
are breathing a virgin atmosphere.... To be the
first – that is the idea. To do something, say
something, see something, before anybody else –
these are the things that confer a pleasure compared with which other pleasures are tame and
commonplace, other ecstasies cheap and trivial.

Mark Twain in *Innocents Abroad*

I never considered myself to be an explorer in the geographic sense, of course. I knew perfectly well that
others had preceded me in the body. This was not neces-
sarily the case, however, with respect to perception and
appreciation. There is a strange magic about the red-rock
country that encourages the conviction in every visitor
that he or she is the first human being ever to see what
lies before the eye.

One explanation for this peculiar effect is that the
wild and extremely rugged nature of the landscape - as

well as its constantly changing imagery, indeed its very
ineffableness - allow each viewer to claim a most personal, individual, **unique** experience of discovery.  That
may very well be the spell under which I fell those long
years ago.

.  .  . Another trip with Bill in the summer of 1946
was eventful.  Before leaving home, we switched wheels on
the old Packard and repaired the gas gauge, generator and
carburetor.  Bill cashed three of his war bonds and I
pawned my binoculars for $20 (so critical was our financial
situation).  In Grass Valley near Fish Lake, 170 miles
south of Salt Lake City, we had the first tire blowout.
It was "A humdinger which ruined the tire but not the
tube."  A used replacement was purchased in Bicknell
for $4.

That night we slept in the car beside the abandoned rock
building at Giles, in Blue Valley east of Caineville.  The
desolate clay landscape, so hauntingly beautiful to me
now, was depressing then.  We were fearful about going on
because of our undependable car.  East of Torrey, at that
time and for years to come, the road was unpaved, often
rutted, and almost impassable in places when wet.

South of Hanksville the road crossed the sandy wastes
of Burr Desert.  Peaks of the Henry Mountains dominated
both land and sky.  At that time I knew little about the
Henrys.  Compared with the Wasatch they were not overly
impressive mountains, though almost as high.  Their aura
eventually brightened as I learned about their unusual
geological structure, the origin of their name, scientific
explorations, and romantic stories about gold mining,
English ranching, and outlaw rustlers.  Today I regard
them as noble landmarks, fascinating for their geological
uniqueness and beauty of form.  Panoramas from high points
on the Henrys are inspirational.

The road for some 20-odd miles south of Hanksville was
not difficult, having long been a ranching thoroughfare and
the route at one time of gold miners.  Through the deepen-
ing gorge of North Wash, however, it was an abomination.
Only a short time before our trip a bulldozer crew under
the direction of Art Chaffin had bladed and roughly graded
a vehicle path down the wash to the Colorado and Hite.
This was not too bad where creekbed crossings were not
involved, but summer floods always washed away the
approaches to these numerous crossings.  (In later years
I counted some 50 crossings of the creekbed in 15 or 20
miles.)  The roadbuilders hadn't wasted much effort at the

crossings, other than to prepare approaches, knowing what havoc the inevitable floods would wreak.

Loose rocks, sand, ruts, and washes were the order of travel, even on that newly built North Wash road. It was eminently unsuitable for our ponderous Packard, which soon sank into loose sand. Being prepared with burlap sacks and shovel, we extricated the car in due time and proceeded to Hite, about six miles downstream from the mouth of North Wash on the west bank of the river. There we visited Art Chaffin and some of the road crew.

I was aware, rather vaguely, that Chaffin was a legend of sorts, a veteran who knew that country and the river as well as anyone. Though somewhat discouraged by that time with the prospects of vehicle touring, I was coming under the spell of the Colorado River and Glen Canyon.

We asked Chaffin about the feasibility of motor boat trips from Lees Ferry to Rainbow Bridge. He replied that such trips were possible with lots of power but that it was a long upstream pull and sometimes the river was quite low. That information – later confirmed from other sources – was not negative enough to discourage me from changing my touring plans from road to river.

Digging out the old Packard, North Wash.

Since paving was completed on U-95 (the Hanksville-North Wash-Blanding highway) during the 1960s and 1970s, hundreds of thousands of travelers have driven through this violently spectacular Glen Canyon country. All but the most negative or blase must be impressed with the grandeur of its cliffs and canyons, the strangeness of its rock forms, the vividness of its color, which assault the eye almost with a physical impact. Today Lake Powell fills Glen Canyon from wall to wall, to a depth of a hundred feet or so in this vicinity. I will always regard that lake as an alien presence, an interloper which does not belong in Glen Canyon.

Few of today's visitors to this part of the red-rock country have personal knowledge of Glen Canyon in its pristine state, before Lake Powell's invasion, when the Colorado flowed swiftly between sculptured red walls and sandy banks that supported forests of willows, tamarisk, cottonwoods, and other growth that gave haven to wild creatures.

There is no way to describe my emotions and Bill's when first we glimpsed that mighty rush of water at the mouth of North Wash. It was a marvel, a wonder that was almost frightening. Hypnotic, it cast on me a spell of romance that never has released its hold. And the hurt of

Glen Canyon near Hite before drowning by Lake Powell.

Lake Powell, though rationalized and repressed, will
never cease for me.

Returning to Hanksville that afternoon, we had trouble
getting up grades, either from low gas or bad fuel pump.
"Just to be safe, we coasted most of the last 28 miles into
Hanksville, where we filled up at 30¢ a gallon. It was
nearly dark then, so we stopped beside the road several
miles west of Hanksville for the night and our supper -
soup for me, chili for Bill."

Next morning our bad tire blew out near Notom. Nearly
all of our hot and cold patch failed to stop the leak;
another patch was required in Capitol Gorge. We bought
supplies in Torrey, intending to abort our trip and
return home because of so much tire and fuel pump trouble.
But plans are changed often by local advice: the colorful description of the route over Boulder Mountain, given
to us by a rancher near Torrey, influenced us to do what
we had originally intended to do.

I have always favored the name Aquarius Plateau as
being more appropriate and dignified than the prosaic
Boulder Mountain, a more commonly used synonym. Whatever
the name, views from the heights of this grand uplift
must rank high on any list of superlative-sublime scenic
experiences to be had in the world. Or, at least, on a
list of scenic experiences of the Aquarius Plateau type,
namely an incredible variety of landforms, types of rocks,
geological structures, and vibrantly diversified colors,
extending from one's feet to landmarks 80 or 100 miles
away.

This first journey around the eastern and southern
shoulders of the Aquarius was a profound continuation of
my awakening process. It shook Bill and me to our depths,
and though both of us visited many other places in years
to come, our initial awe remained to color everything we
viewed in future.

It was my first overview acquaintance with the Waterpocket Fold, the Circle Cliffs wilderness, the heavenly
white slickrock slopes and gorges of the upper Escalante.
The sunken basin of the lower Escalante dominated the
middleground to the south, its ethereal features tanta-
lizingly indistinct.

Far away beyond that basin was Navajo Mountain, a
mystic dome that overlooked Navajoland, Glen Canyon,
Rainbow Bridge, the canyoned Colorado: names, places and
concepts that thrilled me with their connotations of wild-

ness and remoteness, unbelievable ruggedness, adventure, exploration, sheer beauty.

Away to the west and southwest, joining Navajo Mountain visually to the Aquarius, was a long, almost unbroken rampart that – even then, at the beginning of my reading career – I knew was the face of the Kaiparowits Plateau. The mysterious Kaiparowits was described in *Utah: A Guide to the State* in words that could not fail to stir any but the most unromantic heart. Already I had devoured much of that book, my Utah bible.

I knew from the guidebook about the sufferings of the Hole-in-the-Rock pioneers, who had traversed that maze of rainbow rocks more than 60 years before. And about Escalante and Boulder towns, and the Dominguez-Escalante expedition of 1776 which crossed the Colorado near Navajo Mountain, and the Powell expeditions, and the Henry Mountains. All these were subjects of emotional interest to me. So was the Aquarius Plateau itself, which remains one of the favorite mountains in my world.

We left the highway at Teasdale on the unpaved road through Grover. Improved to reasonable graded standards only a few years previously by the CCC, the road climbed and dipped and wound along the steep mountainside, beneath the dark lava platform that crowns the Aquarius.

Aquarius Plateau (Boulder Mountain) from Miners Mountain.

Tantalus Flats and peaks of the Henry Mountains (planed flat by clouds), looking east from Aquarius Plateau.

The summit of the Aquarius is as true a plateau as a landform is likely to be, an expansive "plate" of hard volcanic magma, almost flat and rimmed by 400-foot-high cliffs. On the plateau top and at the base of the cliffs are numerous small lakes and ponds: hence the name Aquarius. Thousand Lake Mountain to the north is a smaller edition of the Aquarius, just as high but with fewer lakes. In its individual way that superb uplift is just as spectacular as the Aquarius.

The road penetrated then, and still does, a lush forest of long-needled ponderosa pines, which tend to be spaced in pleasing openness, alternating with groves of aspen and expansive meadows that permit those tremendous panoramic views that distinguish the Aquarius above all other characteristics.

All went well for 20 miles or so; then, on steep grades, the car balked. We found it necessary to back up as far as possible and make a fast run to the up-grade, using our momentum to help the engine. The generator had not been charging, we found when a dead battery refused to turn the starter. This problem was resolved by a two-

hour wait for the battery to rejuvenate itself enough to
start the car.

We camped near Boulder that night, and in Escalante next
day we charged the battery and bought a tube and patch.
"From there to Widtsoe over the hump we had a bad time the
first half of the climb when Liz conked out, but there I
found out the trouble was vapor lock more than fuel pump.
[In those days the main road west of Escalante climbed
over Escalante Mountain to an altitude of 9,000 feet.
That is now a forest road.]

"After letting her cool off I wrapped a wet towel
around the gas line leading from the fuel pump to the carburetor and had Bill sit on the fender pouring cold water
on it till we got over the summit. It did the trick, too
- not a hitch the last half, which was also the worst
half."

We stopped at Bryce Canyon, the first time for either
of us. If was "more beautiful than anything" we'd seen
on the trip, I wrote. That judgment illustrates a common
trait or tendency toward classifying places and things as
"the most" or "the best". I have been guilty of such
sweeping generalizations, perhaps because of the nature
of my promotional writings. With maturity I have tried to
be more restrained, realizing now that esthetic judgments
and comparisons can only be subjective opinions in the
final analysis. In the case of the Enchanted Wilderness,
it would be absolutely impossible for me to be objec-
tive.

North of Panguitch two more tires blew out in rapid
succession. "By then we were about ready to blow out ourselves, but Bill caught a ride back to the nearest town to
buy another tire and get a tube fixed while I switched the
good tires to the back and the poor ones to the front."
The generator was inoperative, so we slept near the highway a few miles south of Richfield. Another tire blew
near Indianola, conveniently close for me to walk a mile
to our Houtz cousins' house. They provided us with a
booted replacement, and we drove the final 75 miles to
Salt Lake City at 20 miles per hour with only one repair
job along the way.

. . . Those expeditions of the summer of 1946, rather
than satisying my craving to see and learn more about the
red-rock country, only served as appetizers. Anybody with
unrealized longings will know what I mean; and he or she
will understand the frustrations resulting from lack of

money and time, as well as the demands of more pressing obligations such as school, work and family responsibilities. I was enrolled full time at the university, subsisting on a meager income from the government and what I had earned during the summer.

Today I can't explain how I could afford to buy Utah books that winter, but I did begin a collection that eventually amounted to more than 600 titles - books, pamphlets, and miscellaneous items - nearly all of which were on the subject of southern Utah. Also I began a collection of maps and started to compile a southern Utah bibliography and index to my collection. I haunted the city's bookstores, government agencies, the State Historical Society, and other sources, not always buying (I could afford only a few of the items I yearned for) but gaining knowledge of the field.

I had little competition from other collectors at the time. Serious public interest in the Colorado Plateau, the area of my main concern, was in the future. So I could have purchased, if I had had the means, practically any item I wanted at a fraction of what such items would bring only a few years later.

As it turned out, within a year or two I had obtained copies of nearly every first-edition title issued by or referring to the Powell expeditions, including books by Powell himself, Dellenbaugh, Stone, etc. I had the beautiful atlases of Grand Canyon and the High Plateaus by Holmes and Dutton, together with accompanying texts. I had first editions of Gilbert's monographs on the Henry Mountains and Lake Bonneville, and some volumes of the Wheeler and Hayden surveys, and most Geological Survey works having to do with Utah's part of the Colorado Plateau. Hundreds of other titles were in my collection as well. All of these were obtained at a total cost of a few hundred dollars, the sum of my disposable income. Today they would be worth thousands.

Only a few years later, working for my master's degree and being badly in need of funds, I sold many of my books for less than I had paid. Strange to say, I never regretted doing that. They had served their primary purpose, and by that time I had recognized my collecting craze for what it was: an obsession. I was being collected by my collection.

Those years of intense initial fascination with the redrock country in particular and Utah in general introduced me to many interesting people. Among the book dealers I

Morning in the High Plateaus.

became acquainted with Gene Wilson of Wilson's Bookstore, Sam Weller of Zion's, and Mrs. Richard Shepard of Shepard's. From Mrs. Shepard I purchased the majority of my most treasured Powell titles.

Mrs. Shepard and her late husband had known Frederick Dellenbaugh, Powell's artist on his second river expedition and author of books I lusted after. She provided me with first edition copies of those from her own library.

During those years of the late 1940s I became acquainted with Dale Morgan, Charles Kelly, and Albert R. Lyman, historians who awed me (I was a hero worshipper). I became acquainted with a number of river guides. One of my closest friends was Mary Lyman Reeve, sister of Albert R. Lyman, the venerable San Juan chronicler. A Bluff pioneer, Mrs. Reeve was a mentor of mine for years, a grand matriarch whose memory I revere.

That was a stimulating period for the shy, introspective young man I happened to be. Personal relations were not too easy for me outside my circle of family, relatives, and a few close friends. But I lived a rich emotional life through my fascination with a marvelous wilderness which few other people knew about and fewer still had ever seen or cared to visit. Meeting kindred spirits who loved the country I loved was a bonus. Such encounters only spurred my enthusiasm. I could hardly wait for the end of the 1947 spring quarter.

. . . In April 1947 Darrell and I bid on surplus military jeeps at Tooele Army Depot, being among 7,000 other veterans who attended the drawing. Darrell's number was drawn among the first, so he chose the jeep which was first on both our lists. It was a vehicle in good condition. My number was drawn after nearly all jeeps on my list had been sold. I purchased one for $125, a 1943 model with good tires. As we soon discovered, it had a cracked block, bad clutch, and other defects. But once repaired, those little work-horses gave us great pleasure in years to come, taking us over the worst possible roads and tracks into some of the remotest parts of Utah.

A month later, my younger brother Bill and I drove my jeep to Hole-in-the-Rock. We took the Grover-Boulder road over the Aquarius, which had impressed us so greatly the previous year. This was our first traverse of the country south of Escalante. A graded, fair-weather road followed the general route of the Hole-in-the-Rock pioneers who passed through in 1879.

This road was, and is, on the sandy benchland between the Kaiparowits cliff-face (50-Mile Mountain or Straight Cliffs) and tributary washes of the Escalante River. In 1947 it was a fairly good dirt road as far as Rock Corral, about 50 or 60 miles south of Escalante. Beyond there the road disintegrated into elusive tracks that often disappeared into sand traps or onto stretches of slickrock where no trace of wheels could be seen.

Uncertain of the trail ahead I foolishly drove down a steep slope of slickrock into a sandy bowl. Though I stopped as soon as I detected that we were in a sand trap, it was impossible to go backward, even in four-wheel drive. Sand bags and rocks failed to help.

Being late in the afternoon, we decided to leave the jeep there and strike out on foot toward the Hole, which was marked by a prominent cleft or notch in the cliff to the east. The two-mile hike took us an hour or more and we were only able to climb about halfway down the Hole before approaching dusk signaled the wisdom of return to the jeep and our equipment. "The whole country is beautiful—magnificent—and weird," I wrote later, inadequately then as afterwards.

On the way back to the jeep we were tramping along across country when Bill let out a yelp and I stopped. About three feet in front of me was a little sidewinder rattler, coiled ready to strike. We called Curly (our little black cocker spaniel who always accompanied us), to keep him from going up and investigating the snake. Then we took off post-haste because it was almost dark - too dark, in fact, to take our bearings by the time we reached the vicinity of the jeep. Fortunately, by almost feeling our way through that unearthly terrain of mounded slickrock, surreal at any time of day or night, we finally came upon the jeep, or jitney as we called it. Utterly exhausted, we climbed into our sleeping bags without further ado.

(I should note here that in all the hundreds of days I have spent in the red-rock country I have seen only three or four rattlesnakes. This might indicate that I do not notice the obvious; other people claim to come upon snakes rather frequently. Whatever the reason, snakes and I have avoided each other; but even when I see them I let them go their way unmolested if they let me go mine.

Another observation: Night is a dangerous time to walk off-trail or off-road in the red-rock country. Distances cannot be judged accurately, even a few feet away.

It is easy to become disoriented, and there is real danger of falling off a ledge. Years ago I read in the newspaper of a woman who had fallen to her death from a high rim above the Colorado River near Moab. As I recall, she had been riding in a car after dark. The car had pulled to the side of the road and stopped to let her out. Only a few feet from the car, not seeing the abyss in the darkness, she stepped over the edge.)

Next morning we arose at five to size up our situation. We were 65 miles from Escalante and the jeep was sunk in loose sand to the rear axle. It was foolhardy to plunge ahead; there was too much sand in that direction. The jeep was headed downhill and solid slickrock was only a few feet behind it, but because of the slope and sand around the wheels we could not get enough traction to move. To shorten a description of what amounted to five hours of hard digging in blazing heat, we finally succeeded in reaching the slickrock.

This was done by jacking up each wheel and packing the cavity with rocks, canvas, tire chains, brush, or whatever else of a solid nature we could find. Time after time the wheels would just spin everything out and sink deeper into the fine sand.

I wrote later that "By the time we got through – hot, thirsty, raging, and discouraged – we were ready to give up. The heat was terrific, especially when we tried to shovel sand. I must have eaten a dozen oranges. That was the last of our troubles, though. What a trip – and what wonderful country! I sure love it – it's in my blood."

Bill marked the spot with a crude sign reading **"Site of the plight of the Hole-in-the-Sand Pioneers."**

. . . Less than a month later we were on the road again, this time accompanied by our friend Grant Heward, and Curly of course. Our destination was the North Rim of Grand Canyon via southeastern Utah, and from there back to Salt Lake City. We were away from home nine days, traveling a thousand miles. Today the entire distance is paved and there are good motels and restaurants, conveniently spaced along the route. The inspirational scenery has not changed since our journey, of course, though the aura of wild remoteness has dimmed, especially along the main roads.

Our third attempt at finding arches in the Devils Garden section of Arches National Monument failed like the first two attempts. As before, we entered through

Jeeping in the 1940s. Bill stands beside my jeep
at Hole-in-the-Sand, near Hole-in-the-Rock (above).
Darrell, in the second jeep (below) traveled in
comfort and style: he carried his mattress along on
top of his vehicle.

Salt Valley, the present paved route into the Windows
Section being years in the future. That night we camped
in the LaSal Mountains for the first time. A side trip
to Geyser Pass was foiled by snow, but the LaSals did not
disappoint us otherwise. How could they disappoint anybody? I have returned many times to this lovely range
with the perfect peaks. Even the second flat tire of our
trip was viewed with equanimity. We were happy and at
peace in that superlative setting.

> *Once or twice in a lifetime (maybe more than that*
>     *if a person is very fortunate);*
> *In the perfect place, under conditions that may*
>     *never occur again -*
> *Perhaps on a mountain top with the late sun*
>     *breaking through clouds in diffused*
>     *radiance -*
> *Eternity may cease its flow, the world pause,*
>     *for one incomprehensible moment...*
> *An instant in time, to be treasured forever.*

In Moab we bought gasoline, groceries, and ice cream,
then headed south toward Monticello. At the Home of
Truth junction we turned west, past the mostly deserted
buildings of that forlorn religious colony, dropping into
Indian Creek Canyon. "That valley is like a garden of
Eden," I wrote. "Fertile, cool, fresh, and really
delightful." There we talked with some of Scorup's cowboys taking cattle to the LaSals.

At Dugout Ranch we asked J. A. Scorup himself about
the road to Cave Spring. He told us that one of his
pickup trucks had been in there the previous year, and
that a tractor had been right into The Needles. That was
the history-making "cat" that had bulldozed the famous
(or infamous) jeep trail over Elephant Hill, which I later
walked, "totegoted" and jeeped numerous times. Now in
Canyonlands National Park, Elephant Hill is still one of
the most challenging short stretches of four-wheel-drive
terrain in America.

Scorup's name and reputation were familiar to me at
that time. I knew he was a living legend, one of the dis-
coverers of the White Canyon natural bridges who knew the
San Juan wilderness as well as any other person, living or
dead. And I knew about The Needles, if only vaguely
because hardly anything had been published concerning them.
My main source at that time was Professor J. S. Newberry's
intriguing description in Captain Macomb's *Report of An*

*Exploring Expedition from Santa Fe to the Junction of the Grand and Green Rivers in 1859*, published in 1876. New-berry's description (quoted on page 734 of my revised *Utah: A Guide to the State*) was tantalizing enough to justify the entire trip.

Scorup, as I remember him, was a large man with a for-bidding mien. He was not cordial, and I suppose there was no reason he should have been. Those who spend their lives in lonely places are not always pleased with in-truders, and Scorup - though prominent in business and livestock affairs - had probably spent as much time in lonely places as any man of that time or situation. Later, his daughter, a retired librarian in Salina, sent me a printed copy of his biography which she had written. I believe The Needles-Salt Creek country was very dear to him, as it became to me.

We camped that night on Indian Creek near South Six-shooter Peak, a few miles from the site just recently (nearly 40 years later) proposed by the Department of Energy as a nuclear waste repository. We were awed and ecstatic as we bedded down in Canyonlands, on the edge of the most marvelous wilderness we knew, a red fantasy-land which would become a national park some 20 years later.

I cannot conceive of a government of all the people considering even for a moment the placing of a nuclear waste dump in such a location, but I suppose a govern-ment that had exterminated thousands of human beings in a few seconds with nuclear weapons, only two years pre-vious to our visit, would hardly balk at placing such a repository beside a national park.

A big sand dune across the road at Salt Creek blocked our jeep from reaching Cave Spring, so we gathered sup-plies and walked to that rustic cowboy camp. From Cave Spring we tried to find our way into The Needles, dis-covering after several tiring miles that we had taken the wrong trail and were following the bed of Salt Creek.

Next day we found the right trail. We slaked our thirst at Squaw Spring and Soda Spring, then climbed the caterpillar switchbacks over Elephant Hill and threaded the narrow lanes as far as Devils Pocket, about ten miles from the jeep. There, because of the lateness of the day, we turned back for camp.

"Our return was really forced," I wrote. "Curly got so tired he would flop on the sand several times and have

to be helped up some high places. We were still a mile
or more from Cave Spring when darkness fell and Grant had
to lead the way with his flashlight. Bill and I were
just about dead when we finally reached camp. Our walking was perfectly automatic. I never want to go through
that again."

It is just as well to note here that Bill and I were
poor hikers. Our hip joints always had been painful when
overused, though adequate for normal use. Hikes of more
than a few miles were distressful, even agonizing. Both
of us, however, were willing to walk many a mile if those
miles promised a worthwhile experience. Years later we
had our hip joints replaced.

Bill is seven years my junior. He was my companion on
numerous trips into the wilds of the red-rock country.
Bill loved it as I did, if not for exactly the same
reasons. Being an avid disciple of Richard Halliburton,
the storied traveler and idol of countless young people of
our generation, Bill longed for adventure in exotic places.

After his marriage a few years later, in the 1950s,
Bill and his wife Grace embarked for Japan. There they
obtained motor scooters of the bulky Lambretta type and
drove them through Japan, southeast Asia, India, and
Afghanistan. Bill has visited almost every country in
North and South America, as far south as Cape Horn. He
worked his way through University of Utah and is the most
original thinker and dreamer of more wonderful dreams
than anybody else I know.

Grant Heward, the third member of our party, also joined
us on trips through the years. A true "original", Grant
was a self-taught natural linguist. In later years he
learned Chinese, even became an adept reader of ancient
Egyptian, and at the present time is teaching English in
China. Grant's voracity for food as well as knowledge
constantly amazed us, but his unfailing good humor was a
great rejuvenator whenever our spirits sagged.

We left The Needles next morning, but not for the last
time. That incredible sandstone jungle haunted me. No
adequate description of The Needles ever has been written,
to my knowledge. Nor has any writer done descriptive justice to the adjoining Salt Creek labyrinth, or to the
Land of Standing Rocks across the river. These, with The
Needles, are units of a compact, architecturally integrated
region surrounding the confluence of the Green and Colorado rivers.

I am not sure that anybody could come close to conveying in words or on film the peculiar magic of that sacred heart of Canyonlands. So far as I know that area is completely unique, not only in physical characteristics but also because its forms, designs and color combinations are so absolutely alien to the concepts associated with natural phenomena in more familiar places.

They are a new entry in the book of esthetics. Human psychology has not yet adapted to them — or, for that matter, to the art in stone displayed elsewhere throughout the Enchanted Wilderness.

> *Forms that soar from quiet, shaded depths*
> *to aerial majesty;*
> *And by their grandeur seize the heart,*
> *and lead the soul*
> *Through portals of enchantment*
> *to Sublimity.*

Newberry likened the spires of The Needles to the towers of Manhattan. That is a valid comparison, but only in a vague sense, for no skyline built by man matches the mystical skyline of The Needles in delicacy and harmonious variation of line and form, not to mention coloration.

Devils Pocket in The Needles, Canyonlands National
Park. This was my Shangri-la.

The rock forms of this area simply are beyond count or
classification, for they change into something different
with every repositioning of perspective, however minute,
whether the viewer moves backward or forward, up or down,
left or right. Every exquisitely contoured form or slope
flows magically into adjoining forms or slopes; all of
these together combine into an inorganic masterpiece that
cannot be fully appreciated from the ground alone, or from
any single high place, or even from a moving airplane –
or, for that matter, from any fixed points, however numerous and varied. All perspectives are necessary for appreciation. Appreciation is dependent, also, on personal
moods, seasons, weather, and hours of the day.

I knew then that I could never exhaust the visual and
emotional treasury of The Needles, but I tried to do so
with repeated visits over the coming years. Even then I
could write, "Some day this area will be as well known as
Bryce and Zion, probably, although now even people around
here don't know what the Needles are."

Thank heaven that prophecy has not come true. I hope
it never does. It never could, of course. The very ruggedness and isolation of the area will prevent that, at

least for years to come.  And this may be its salvation
from people pollution.  Industrialization is another
matter.

We bathed in Indian Creek and stopped in Blanding for
gasoline, ice cream and staples.  "I asked Bill and Grant
to get us some things we needed, so they came back with
four rolls of toilet paper (we needed one, I'll admit)
and a lot of onions."

Bluff was the most desolate, scorched town any of us
had seen.  "What those poor settlers must have gone
through," I noted then.  I have never had much reason to
change that opinion of its physical appearance, though it
does possess a romantic mystique.

That night we camped at the Goosenecks overlook.  Curly
had not recovered from The Needles hike.  His paws were
paining him and he showed no animation at all.

In Monument Valley we saw the western movie set at
Goulding's Junction.  Erected a few years previously for
"My Darling Clementine", it consisted of a few corral
posts and building facades.  We did not stop at the
trading post.

Every part of the red-rock country has its own personality, and each must be appreciated on its own merits.
Of course, we all have personal preferences.  After experiencing Dead Horse Point and The Needles, I personally
found Monument Valley an emotional anticlimax.  There is
no denying its majesty and hypnotic allure.  I have
returned many times, and in fact have developed a greater
affection for that strange place in later years.

The wind blew fiercely in Monument Valley and almost
all the way to Tuba City.  We had no side curtains, hence
little protection from the blowing sand and dust.  Visibility was very poor.  Through Monument Valley and beyond,
sand clogged the road, making for hard pulling even in
the jeep.  Even between areas of sand the road was the
worst we'd ever been on.  "They ought to take the abominable thing off the map," I complained.  We were not
seasoned explorers willing to undergo discomfort passively.

Not finding a camping spot at Jacobs Lake, we drove on
to North Rim campground at Grand Canyon, where we arrived
about 10 p.m.  Bill and I hit the sack immediately, but
Grant - never too tired to eat - built a fire and cooked
his dinner.  That night it rained and snowed for hours.  I
kept warm and dry with raincoat, overcoat and leather

jacket over my bedding, and Grant was all right. Bill, however, was less fortunate. After his sleeping bag became soaked, he took refuge in the freezing latrine for hours.

We traveled through rain all the 400 miles back to Salt Lake City in our open-sided jeep, arriving home with two gallons of gas in the tank and 50 cents in cash between us.

That was our first trip to Grand Canyon. Of course we were awed. I have a photo of Grant and Bill, disheveled, shivering on a viewpoint. Since then I have returned to Grand Canyon many times, to both north and south rims.

My impressions, I'm sure, resemble those of other viewers sensitive to plateau scenery and grand dimensions. My own experience has always been colored by a knowledge of Powell's expeditions and the exploits of river runners who came after; also by personal acquaintance with people who have boated the Colorado through Grand Canyon, either as passengers or crew. But Gloria and I have never boated it ourselves. Of course we would love to traverse that indescribable gorge.

. . . After our return on June 21, 1947, I delivered portrait coupons for Broadway Studio, acting as a deliveryman (using my jeep), then later hiring lady telephone solicitors to sell the coupons, which I delivered and collected the money for. It was a cooperative endeavor, with many hands dipping in the pool, but I managed to clear several hundred dollars.

Also I found time to write a travel article on The Needles, which was published the following spring by the *Salt Lake Tribune*. I received $15 as payment and was ecstatic. That was my first published work. And it was, I believe, the first popular travel piece ever written about The Needles.

Over the Labor Day weekend a group of us tried to reach Halls Crossing on the Colorado River via Halls Creek, which drains the south end of the Waterpocket Fold below Capitol Reef. Bill, Grant and I were in the party, which included my brothers Darrell and Byron, and my cousin Garth Remington. We traveled in our two jeeps.

At Notom we were told that chances of reaching the river were slim, but we were advised to check at ranches down the Fold. Since it was Saturday we found nobody at the ranches. We decided to take our chances and proceed.

The road was bad, rutted, with pockets of sand, and it required innumerable crossings of the creek (Sandy Wash

north of Bitter Creek Divide, Halls Creek to the south).
I noted in my journal that the Waterpocket Fold was
"quite fascinating with its twisted, tortured, convulsive
erosion." The road, more accurately a trail, followed
the valley between the Fold and outrigger mesas of the
Henry Mountains.

Anybody who has driven through that country knows its
grandeur. Cretaceous cliffs on the east rise in terraces,
the broken fronts of great platforms. Forming a solid
wall to the west, the Waterpocket Fold is an immense spine
of naked, steeply tilted, varicolored, beautifully sculptured sandstone. The Fold is a narrow monoclinal uplift
extending about 80 miles in a north-south direction
between Thousand Lake Mountain and Glen Canyon. Capitol
Reef is the best known part of the Fold, almost the entire
length of which is now included in Capitol Reef National
Park and Glen Canyon National Recreation Area.

The Fold's great whaleback ridge rises above the valley
to heights of more than a thousand feet in places. Innumerable dead-end canyons and slots provide delightful
hiking and climbing possibilities.

On the second day we stopped at one place where there
was an ascending series of waterpockets, some of them

My jeep stuck in quicksand, Halls Creek, Waterpocket
Fold (below). Still stuck (opposite).

quite deep with clear, drinkable water.  Not far beyond
these we came to a streambed crossing which looked no
different than many others we had traversed.

Byron was driving my jeep, following Darrell's.  There
was no flowing water, and the moist sand of the creek
bottom looked innocent enough.  Darrell plunged across
with no trouble, but the second jeep, following in his
tracks at a slower speed, bogged down to the floorboard
in what we soon discovered was quicksand.

There was no budging my jeep, even with a chain attached
to Darrell's.  With all of us helping to dig, it took
nearly three hours of hard work to escape.  Each corner
of the body and every wheel were jacked up, using the spare
wheel as a jack base, and wheel foundations were built of
rocks.  Then, with my jeep in low compound and a jerk by
Darrell, we pulled out.

Not far beyond that spot we stopped finally at the
edge of a five-foot ledge above the creekbed.  Scouting
ahead, we saw that there was too much water and quicksand
for our tastes.  We decided to turn back, not with great
regret because the trail evidently hadn't been used for
years by any wheeled vehicle.  In many places we lost it

altogether.  "Without exaggeration," I noted, "it was the
worst road we've ever tackled."

Our turnabout point was about 55 miles south of Notom,
far beyond the present Burr Trail switchbacks and not too
many miles from the river.  Most of our route south of
the Burr Trail is now within a designated park wilderness.

That night we camped beside some deep waterpockets and
had a refreshing bath.  Several of us climbed the smooth
slopes of the Fold next morning, attempting to reach the
crest, only to be frustrated by "enormous canyons, invis-
ible from the valley but plenty visible above."  We
arrived home the same night, thoroughly fed up with bad
roads.

. . . It was rarely possible for us to spend more than
three days on these excursions.  Three days were a necessary minimum, however, because of distances involved.
Nearly all our destinations were from 200 to 300 miles
from Salt Lake City, some even farther.  Three days
allowed us only one full day and parts of the other two
days within the area proper - hardly enough time for much
exploration on foot.  We always left for home unfulfilled.
At the same time, we were weary, dirty, and tired of heat,
gnats, sand, dust, car troubles, and rough roads.  Except
for yearning, which never ceased, three days at a time
usually sufficed for me.

My brothers Bill and Darrell joined me most frequently.
As I mentioned, Bill had a deep love for the red-rock
country, or more accurately was entranced by its wild
romance.  Other elements were involved in my own love
affair.

Darrell, two years my junior, craved adventure of any
kind.  A Navy veteran who had spent two years on an LST
in the Pacific (Curly, his dog, was ship's mascot), Darrell was a mechanical innovator without peer.  Many times,
in the most remote places and under the most adverse conditions, he would repair seemingly hopeless mechanical
breakdowns.  In later years he preferred boating to
jeeping.  I didn't blame him.  Travel on rough roads never
was an end in itself even for me.  It was merely a means
of reaching a goal, a hard way to have an adventure.

. . . Later in 1947, on a September weekend, I returned
to The Needles.  This time, except for Curly, I was alone.
Leaving home shortly after midnight, I drove all night
and arrived at Salt Creek in mid-afternoon.

That night was the loneliest I ever spent. I found the silence and emptiness oppressive. I was not used to being alone in the wilderness, and many solo trips in future never accustomed me fully to such utter solitude. Staring into the black infinity above - thinking about death, eternity, immortality - I was frightened and halfway expectant of something I could not formulate.

At that time I was an agnostic, uncertain of the religious tenets I had been taught and having no replacement philosophy. Subsequent reading and personal experiences answered many of my questions. Eventually, on a lonely pilgrimage, I received the spiritual testimony that has never needed reassurance in all the years since. That profound religious experience was what I had expected on other lonely nights, I suppose, though its initial impact did not come at night under a starry sky.

Next day I arose early "after one **silent** night". Taking a pack, I walked as far as Squaw Spring. By then my hips were so painful I had to turn back. Still, I could write that "I feel now more than ever that this country is destined for a great future as far as scenery is concerned."

The Needles had established a priority position in my affections. I returned time and time again in later years. I dreamed of a little cabin retreat - even a guest ranch where I could show other people the most marvelous place in the world. Investigating land ownership, I found to my delight that Devils Pocket - the scenic heart of The Needles, as I thought at the time - was part of a state school section. I applied to the State Land Board for lease or purchase. It would have to be visited and appraised, I was told. That would take time, and it did take time - too much time, in fact. Before an appraisal was ever made I had given up hope and was dreaming of other things.

(Some time later I became acquainted with Kent and Fern Frost of Monticello, who made their living for years taking people into The Needles and other remote parts of the red-rock country. Kent loved The Needles and Standing Rocks beyond any other place, I believe. He spent long periods alone in that sandstone maze, hiking, exploring, climbing cliffs and forbidding heights that I could not attempt. I have always envied and admired Kent and Fern. They personify that region for me, insofar as it can be personified. Kent described his geographical love affair in *My Canyonlands*.)

Returning to the highway from The Needles, I talked for a few minutes with a young fellow who was herding turkeys for Scorup. "He's from Minnesota or Wisconsin," I noted, "and seems to like this country. He must - he's alone nearly all the time." I camped that night in Cooley Pass in the Abajo Mountains, between Abajo and Horsehead peaks. It was very cold. At the crack of dawn I arose, and after packing I tried to climb Horsehead Peak. Not being very agile, I was fearful of the loose rock and did not reach the top. But that high vantage point added to my general excitement.

I drove on to the south side of the range to where I could get a panoramic overview of the entire Four Corners region: south to Comb Ridge, Grand Gulch, Monument Valley ... east to Ute Mountain and the Rockies of Colorado ... west to Elk Ridge, the Henry peaks, and those unearthly breaks of the Colorado River. I was not altogether familiar with the topographical relationships before me, but I knew enough for orientation.

And I knew enough history to be enthralled at the thought of the human dramas that had played out on that magnificent stage. Pioneers and settlers eking out a hard livelihood ... the prehistoric Ancient Ones ... Indians and traders ... cowboys and sheepherders ... gunfighters and lawmen ... soldiers ... miners ... explorers ... geologists.

I had read about them all. My heart overflowed. The enchantment continued, and I returned home in high spirits, still hoping that my destiny would be entwined with that of the red-rock country....

. . . . That winter of 1947-48, with my brothers, I purchased an outboard engine and two rubber rafts: a heavy seven-man Navy assault raft for $27 and a lightweight seven-man Air Force raft for $15. We had decided to boat the Colorado River through Glen Canyon. I also purchased a second-hand 16mm movie camera, which became an indispensable adjunct to future expeditions as well as the recorder of Christmas gatherings of our clan for many years.

I interviewed Don Harris about our plans to boat the river and transport tourists upstream from Lees Ferry to Rainbow Bridge. He thought it was possible, and of course it was. Art Greene did that very thing for years, though I am not sure just when he started to do so; regardless, we were not aware of competition at that time.

Don Harris was a water engineer employed by the U. S. Geological Survey. He was friendly and helpful on my first visit. Years later I got to know Don well, and his wife Mary. Don was respected as one of the most able and knowledgeable rivermen on the Green and Colorado. He took no chances. He knew the rivers, their eccentricities and dangers. He could be trusted.

Bill and I attended a public showing of Al Morton's 16mm film on his boat trip from Moab to Lees Ferry. The film only strengthened my resolve to start a boat-tour business in Glen Canyon. Eventually I came to know Al Morton well. He and Thelma, his wife, became our close friends.

Al was a postal lettercarrier who gained quite a reputation as "The movie-making mailman". Though his 16mm repertoire was not confined to travel, Al's entertaining river films were especially popular. They were pioneering documentaries, classics of their kind, immortalizing an era of hard-hull cataract boats. During the 1950s and 1960s I accompanied Al on a number of river trips in Utah and Mexico.

For our Glen Canyon venture we planned to build a special shallow-draft boat, 18 feet long, powered by a Ford Model A engine and driven by an air propeller. Even Darrell was enthusiastic. During that winter of 1947-48 we discussed power boats and how to adapt them to the Colorado in Glen Canyon.

In late March of 1948 we embarked on the Colorado at the mouth of North Wash. Our party included myself, Darrell, Byron, Bill, Grant Heward, and Darrell's little dog Punky. My brother Duane and friend LeRoy Nelsen accompanied us as return drivers. Only Darrell had boating experience.

We left Salt Lake City in our two jeeps, pulling a trailer, accompanied by snow, bitter cold, and the usual assortment of mechanical troubles: a flat tire and broken valve spring before we reached Mount Pleasant, a hundred miles along the way. That night seven of us slept in one motel room, after working on the tires and valve until 1 a.m. Next morning the water pump and rear wheels on Darrell's jeep were frozen tight, requiring two hours for thawing.

In Hanksville we found the reason for my jeep's losing water and overheating: the head gasket was leaking water into the oil. All the way to the river we added water to the radiator. The road through North Wash to the river, in the dark, seemed endless and unendurably rough. The river, when we finally reached it, "was spooky in the moonlight - and seemed to move awfully fast." I still feel strong emotion when I recall that great surge of water rushing past our sandy campsite that first night.

Duane and LeRoy left next morning with the jeeps, taking "our best wishes but few hopes". After loading - a task that required hours and much ingenuity - we shoved off, the heavy neoprene raft with outboard towing the lighweight raft. At Hite we talked with Art Chaffin and a boater who had just come 60 miles upstream with a 22-horsepower outboard. The river was easy to take, he said.

Our trip of 168 miles to Lees Ferry required five days. At that time of year (March 22-27) the water was low, and even in our shallow-draft craft we had considerable trouble with sandbars. I have a photo of Grant standing hardly more than ankle-deep in the middle of the river. Eventually we learned to avoid most sandbars by following the current around the outside of curves. This, however, did not always succeed.

Apparently we were the first boaters through the length of Glen Canyon that year. Explorer Scouts and others had been boating that stretch since the end of the war, and increasing hundreds, perhaps even thousands, saw Glen Canyon from the river before the invasion of Lake Powell began in the early 1960s. All who did became members of a privileged clique.

Glen Canyon in its primeval beauty was a natural wonder of the world, a continual Zion Canyon in miniature, 190 miles of glorious red cliffs ornamented with an endlessly varied assortment of rock forms, relief designs, and color tapestries.

There were miles of sandy beaches and dense willow forests. Dozens of sheer-walled side canyons and narrow slots in the cliffs invited exploration; some of them contained prehistoric ruins and rock art. There were beaver, deer, birds and other wild creatures. There were old log cabins, the Stanton dredge, Hole-in-the-Rock, Halls Crossing, and Old Ute Ford where the Dominguez-Escalante expedition crossed the river in 1776. Those sites are all buried now by water and muck.

We had no singular "adventures" of thrilling type during those priceless days. Yet there were memorable incidents, and in ways the entire trip was a real adventure. Glen Canyon had no severe rapids, only riffles, but there

were formidable sand waves that threatened to swamp our
little rafts. At times the wind was ferocious. Blowing
sand and spray harried us. We were nearly always cold,
even in the sun. The silty water and wind soon ruined our
complexions. Sandbars, quicksand and willow thickets
discouraged casual side-canyon exploration.

Below Hole-in-the-Rock a strong wind created such big
waves that we made an early camp, the lack of a sandy
beach or level ground forcing us high up the slope among
boulders at the base of the cliffs. There we spent an
uncomfortable night with a terrific gale, blowing sand
and rain.

Near the mouth of Aztec Creek we encountered the worst
wind and waves of the trip. They frightened us: we had
difficulty pulling to shore and making camp. Dusk was
upon us by the time we hiked to Rainbow Bridge, six
miles from the river, allowing no time to linger and savor
the atmosphere of that shrine. Returning, we literally
stumbled the last four miles by flashlight. "They were
terrible, agonizing miles - at least for me and Bill. I
got so I could hardly control my leg movements and would
almost fall over."

Some miles above Lees Ferry we saw the proposed dam
site, and a fellow at the Ferry told us the dam was sched-
uled to be built as soon as money was available.

That news shattered our dream of a boating business in
Glen Canyon. We pursued it no further. More than 20
years elapsed before I attempted to establish another tour
business in the red-rock country.

While at Lees Ferry, unloading and waiting for our
return cars to arrive, we spent hours with an old-timer
who wandered up. He impressed me so much that I wrote
about him at more length than was customary in my journals:

> He was "Red Wolf" - Willard Jim Dale - about 80
> years old. An old squaw man who's been wandering
> over the southwest for ages. First man through
> the Grand Canyon on foot - originator of the
> Arizona "Grand Canyon State" slogan. A queer old
> guy - crippled from a horse accident some years ago
> - long beard and hair. Living in an old shack and
> hogan near Johnson's Ranch and having a hard time
> of it. He told us a lot of experiences fighting
> Mexicans; amorous affairs with Ute squaws, etc.,
> etc. - some of which may have been true. He also
> played on his tom-toms and Ute Bear Dance instrument

(a toothed stick rubbed with a bone, one end of
stick held and the other resting on a tin box). We
visited him this evening at his hogan.

Duane, his wife Virginia, and mother came for us at
2 a.m., having had difficulty finding Lees Ferry. The
400-mile return drive was uneventful except for the
stretch between Payson and Salt Lake City. "That was hell
because of the traffic; scared us to death." Today's
drivers, who complain about freeway congestion, would have
appreciated even less the infuriating stop-and-go congestion on US 91 through Utah and Salt Lake valleys before
Interstate 15 was opened.

. . . Over the Memorial Day weekend of 1948 Bill and I
returned to the San Rafael Swell, driving into Sinbad
(the center of the Swell) to the vicinity of Eagle Canyon — probably as far south as the future I-70. Cowboys
were bringing their cattle off the winter range. Being
ignorant of the consequences, we camped at dusk near a
large herd of cows. That was "One night we'll never forget. Those cows made so much noise we hardly got any
sleep — then a lot of cowboys came about 5 or so and took
them out." The next night we camped in Huntington
Canyon.

Even today the San Rafael Swell is one of the least
known parts of Utah, insofar as the traveling public is
concerned. Millions of car-bound tourists have passed
through the Swell on I-70, catching only glimpses of the
wonders to be found in its precipice-ringed interior and
the recesses of its encircling reef. The Swell's great
buttes are among the most splendid examples of their type
on the Plateau. Canyons of the San Rafael and Muddy
rivers are true spectacles, as are Buckhorn Draw, Eagle
Canyon and other sandstone defiles. Hondoo Country's
cliffs stand in a class by themselves for grandeur. It is
no wonder the Swell captivated me then and has done so
since. Despite numerous return trips over the years, I
have seen only a part of what I know is there to be appreciated. For me the Swell is a discovery reserve, not to
be exhausted in this lifetime.

. . . There were other probings of the red-rock country
during 1948 and 1949, though university classwork and a
half-time job with the State Industrial Commission pre-
vented as much travel as I would have liked. My travels
were not restricted to southern Utah. There were trips to
the east coast, California, Idaho, Wyoming, and the Uinta

Basin of Utah. But I was oppressed by work and responsibility, and I was restless.

When recruiters for the State Department's Foreign Service came to Salt Lake City in May of 1949, I attended
their presentation and applied for a staff position. Not
only was I restless; I was aimless and dissatisfied as
well. "School is horribly boring for me," I wrote. "I've
had so much of it the past ten years, and my job is about
as bad. Guess the army ruined me as it did so many as far
as being content with a routine, secure, uneventful existence is concerned. Maybe I want to run away."

India was my first choice for assignment, North Africa
second. Those were only preferences; we would go where
needed. I waited all summer for acceptance, which hadn't
come before it was necessary to begin fall term and prac-
tice teaching in Granite School District. When the call
did come at the end of September, I was in a quandary. The
telegram left me weak.

Offered salary wasn't high and I had only two quar-
ters at the university before graduation. Other factors
influenced me against accepting. But I did accept, and
within two weeks I was in Washington, studying at the
Foreign Service Institute.

Not having a college degree and not knowing a foreign
language, my position was modest. I studied cryptography
and Foreign Service administration. On December 18 I
landed in Hanoi, North Vietnam, five days after leaving
New York City. I had been in a bed three times in nine
days.

The Vietnam experience has no place in my red-rock
odyssey except indirectly. It conditioned profoundly the
way I looked at Utah, the world, and life in general.
Those 15 months were stressful and wonderful. They solidified the international perspective begun during my Army
years. I returned home convinced that the world must become
unified in myriad ways; that was our planet's only hope
and ultimate future. Also I fell in love with the orient,
its people and culture.

One of the most eventful periods of my life, that was
also one of the most miserable. The Hanoi consulate was
only a small outpost - a satellite of the legation in
Saigon - but in significant ways it was a microcosm of the
entire diplomatic universe. China came under full control
of the Communists just before I arrived. North Korea
invaded South Korea while I was in Hanoi, bringing United

States involvement in that war. And the French were battling the Vietminh throughout the countryside around Hanoi.

Technically I was the consulate's code clerk and
secretary. In effect my position was more important than
it might have been under normal circumstances. Soon after
I arrived the United States began an economic and military
involvement in Indochina that was to culminate in the
great war of the 1960s and 1970s. Even then we could
detect, to our sorrow, what was likely to transpire, for
we saw all around us the morass in which the French were
floundering. We prayed that our country would avoid the
same trap. To us it was obvious that America's leaders
were learning little from French experience. When I
returned to Utah I wrote several papers on that subject
and tried to get them published. There was little public
interest in Vietnam at that time, and I was unsuccessful.

Our consulate hosted a swarm of dignitaries from the
United States, France and Vietnam. There were governors,
generals, ministers, chiefs of mission, economic
advisers, foreign correspondents - even the American
ambassador-at-large, Philip Jessup. While romantic and
exhilarating in their way, those visits and the esca-
lating/deteriorating military situation in North Vietnam
meant a heavy workload for all of us. I approached a
nervous breakdown before additional personnel arrived to
assist me.

In Hanoi I had numerous friends, among them many Viet-
namese and Chinese. My social schedule was overcommitted.
Still I was desperately homesick and unhappy. There were
too many emotional and physical stimuli, too many exotic
and moral choices, for an unsophisticated person with a
restrictive religious and social background. While I had
already lost some of my formal faith, I had little inclination to change my personal habits. There was conflict,
and old attitudes succumbed to new influences at times.

That, then, was a traumatic period. When, early in
1951, I learned that veterans who were not enrolled in
college by a certain date would lose their entitlement
benefits, I decided to resign and return home. This I
did, enrolling again at the University of Utah for spring
quarter. I received my B.S. degree the following year
while working on requirements for an M.S.

. . . It is worth describing one final episode that
occurred during that period of initial red-rock discovery.
Over the Memorial Day holiday of 1952 Bill, Grant and I

returned to The Needles for a more extensive exploration.
We were accompanied by our friends Nyle Walton, Gary Ranck,
and Richard Tham. I brought along a bicycle, hoping to use
it as a carrier and for riding where possible. As it
turned out, there was too much sand for riding, and even
pushing the bike was hard work. We set up camp at Soda
Spring, then hiked over Elephant Hill.

Nyle, Gary and Dick left us in Elephant Canyon, planning to reach the rim of the Colorado River canyon near
its confluence with the Green and return to camp before
dark. Bill, Grant and I hiked into Devils Pocket and
over to Devils Lane. There we decided to return to camp,
being hot, tired and low on water.

Dusk arrived and the others had not returned. We were
very concerned, knowing they had little water and food,
and no camping equipment. After dark, carrying canteens
and sleeping bags, we followed their trail down Elephant
Canyon by moonlight and flashlight. We must have walked
five miles. It was no use; we did not meet them. We spent
a cold night in Elephant Canyon, returning to camp early
in the morning.

Gary and Nyle came loping in about 9 o'clock, saying
Dick was not far behind. They had reached the cliff edge
above the upper Colorado the previous afternoon. Being
out of water and almost mad with thirst, they had no
choice but to descend the precipice to the river. That
was a dangerous feat, in the process of which they barely
avoided serious injury. At the river they drank and swam,
then hiked downstream to the confluence. By nightfall
they were part way back to camp, but too far to reach it,
and they spent a cold night without sleeping bags.

Dick failed to appear. None of us could imagine why,
as Gary and Nyle had left him only a few hundred yards
away on top of Elephant Hill. Gary and Nyle went back
along the trail for a mile or two. No Dick and no sign
of him. Being out of water, they returned to camp.

Grant and I, carrying a canteen, finally found Dick's
tracks leading north along Elephant Canyon toward the
river. That was completely illogical; we knew he must
have been lost or confused. Rushing ahead rather frantically and shouting, I followed his tracks into a side
canyon. There, quite suddenly, about half a mile up the
canyon, I came upon Dick. He was under a tree, wild-
eyed, half delirious from thirst, heat and weariness.

What had happened to him might have happened to anybody

in his condition. Only half a mile from camp but not
knowing that, being tired and thirsty, he had taken shade
under a tree and dozed off. When he awoke, confused by
sleep and the rugged terrain, he retraced the path in the
direction from which he had just come.

None of us laughed. There was twisted humor in the
situation, but it had been too near tragedy to be funny.
Anybody familiar with that fantastic rock jungle can
appreciate Dick's situation perfectly.

Angel Arch                              Broken Bow Arch

# Part Two

# DISCOVERY: THE STATE

The seven years following my return from Indochina in 1951, I suppose, were conditioning for the next period of approximately similar length. They brought a potpourri of experiences, seemingly unrelated to an extent but developmental in sum.

It seems I have always made important decisions according to circumstances of the moment. If a door opens on an opportunity which I deem propitious at the time, I enter. This may appear to be a wishy-washy approach to life, and certainly it would not be suitable for everybody, especially those with family and career responsibilities. I have held many jobs, most of them for only a brief time. So there have been no formal career directions in my life, in the sense of long-term employment with job security and longevity perquisites.

Yet, in a definite sense, I have had a real career. That career has been the exposition of the UTAH concept. For more than forty years I have traveled, studied, written about, photographed, loved and idealized UTAH.

Has it all been worthwhile? Does one small part of the world (only one-sixth of one percent of the earth's land surface, I once calculated) justify a lifetime's devotion? I believe so. Or perhaps I should say that one part of Utah has justified for me a lifetime's career.

## FOUNDATIONS OF A CAREER

After graduating from the University of Utah in 1952 with a teaching certificate in elementary education, I accepted employment with the Salt Lake City Board of Education. I was assigned to teach two 6th grades and two 7th grades.

My career as a classroom teacher was brief and traumatic. I started teaching in September and resigned the

following January, never to return. An ignoble retreat
it was, somewhat comical in retrospect, but I knew almost
immediately I was not cut out to be a classroom teacher.

Since then I rationalize that I have always continued
as a teacher, through the creation of instructional materials which have been used at one time or another in
nearly all the state's schools.

Immediately I embarked on the first of what eventually
was to be a series of publications on Utah and the intermountain west. That was my *Rainbow Roads Guide to Highways 91-89-191*. I soon learned it was sheer madness to
have attempted a project of that magnitude with such
limited financial means and so much inexperience. However,
by the time I became aware of that, I was past the point
of no return. (Since that time Highway 91 has been largely
superseded by Interstate 15.)

I learned several expensive lessons from that book, and
they cost me more than a year of desperate money-scroung-
ing, research, map-making, travel, writing, proofreading,
printer-hassle, face-to-face selling (which I abhorred),
and direct-mail solicitation.

Eventually, several years after the book was published -
being disillusioned, hurt and disappointed (and somewhat
bitter, for I believed that my 250-page book, however
imperfect, was worthwhile) - I took the unbound remainder
of my stock to the flats east of Great Salt Lake and burned
the entire lot.

That symbolic cleansing was therapeutic. Nevertheless,
my self-image - never high anyway - suffered a blow from
which it did not recover for years.

In time I concluded that the Rainbow Roads experience
was a valuable education. Not least on the list of benefits was the concentrated course in the geography, history
and culture of Utah, southern California, southern Nevada,
and eastern Idaho, as well as Grand Canyon and Yellowstone.

Rainbow Roads was the first real application in published form of what I had seen and learned about the intermountain west during the first three decades of my life.
I learned cartography and practiced writing (at least my
writing did not shame me). And what I learned about book
preparation and publishing was invaluable in later years.

The next few years were a dark age which I recall with
pain. Not that this period was uneventful or nonproduc-
tive: it was, in fact, among the most significant of my

life. There were interludes of unemployment, and even the jobs I had were stressful and unfulfilling. There were severe problems of varying nature, strong yearnings, frustrations, indecision.

Yet that was a rich and ecstatic period in ways. We sold our home near Liberty Park and used the proceeds to buy a lot on 25th East, just west of Foothill Boulevard. That foothill area was just beginning to develop, and our lot was a choice scenic parcel. We used it as security for a building loan, with which we built a rambler-type house. Darrell, who also built his own house at that time not far away, supervised the construction.

Our house overlooked the inspirational panorama of Salt Lake Valley, and the beauty of its views gave us much joy during the few years we stayed there. But its cost was too high, financially and in other ways. Several years after moving in we traded our equity for a smaller bungalow in the Sugar House area.

Before that move back down the hill, however, those bird's-eye views from the foothills had captivated me. From our windows on 25th East we could see the entire valley, much of the lake, and mountains as far away as Nevada. Lights of the city at night were magical, and anyone old enough to remember sunsets over Great Salt Lake when the valley's air was relatively clean will agree that they were exceptionally magnificent.

However dramatic, the view from our lot on 25th East did not compare with the tremendous panoramas offered by Olympus Cove. Karl Hale had purchased or optioned a large acreage of grassland in that beautiful aerie over-looked by Mount Olympus and was selling lots for as little as $3,600. View lots today cost as much as a house did in those days.

In the mid-1950s only a few new houses had yet been built in the cove. How I longed to own one of those lots! The view, I thought, would satiate forever my appetite for natural beauty. Many, many times I drove along the newly bladed roads of Olympus Cove, intoxicated by the majesty of the mountain and the valley view, scheming in vain as to how I might find the price of a lot. At times I could not even look at the mountain, being heartsick with long-ing when I saw it.

There was no way I could buy a lot. And later I was glad, for beauty is seldom a joy forever, especially when mortgage payments, taxes, and changing circumstances lurk always on the sidelines.

About this same time the idea of Tour-Tape occurred to me. Magnetic tape was then replacing magnetic wire for recording and playback. I reasoned that millions of tourists were driving America's roads, and particularly in the west they were faced with hours of monotonous open spaces. What a bore! And what a void waiting to be filled with interesting commentary from a prerecorded tape, coordinated with points of geographic and historic interest along those lonely highways. Or so I thought.

I did succeed in interesting several other people, and we formed a corporation. Though we had little capital, we did conduct research that encouraged us as to possibilities and feasibility of the tape theory. Alas, technology defeated us before the overwhelming economic realities would have done so. We found that plug-in or battery-operated playback machines of compact size and reasonable cost were not available, even in prototype.

I now doubt that the psychology of highway sightseers is such that the Tour-Tape concept would be economically viable, although the basic concept is used successfully in some national parks and in many museums. Who can say what the future might bring?

. . . Those years of the 1950s also saw numerous additional probings of the red-rock wilderness, the Wasatch, various parts of the Uintas, the southern parks, western Utah. There were trips to California, Arizona, Idaho, Wyoming.

We brothers looked for a legendary gold mine in the Centennial Mountains between Idaho and Montana. I crossed the Arizona Strip for the first time, saw Betatakin, returned to The Needles several times, drove to Hole-in-the-Rock again. I also joined an official tour to Dead Horse Point.

In June of 1957 I received my M.S. degree from the University of Utah after years of procrastinating the completion of my thesis (which, incidentally, had a Utah theme).

The following month I finally capitulated to ever-stronger spiritual promptings that urged me to go into the wilderness, spending time there alone to study and meditate.

Ten days later I returned home, having experienced religious ecstasy and assurance beyond expectation or description. Those ecstatic promptings were reinforced later on many occasions and from many sources. Never again

did I question that there were profound meanings to life,
and I knew what some of them were in my own case.

## THE TRAVEL COUNCIL ERA

The year 1957 was a landmark in many respects. Of
particular importance was my meeting with D. James Cannon,
director of the Utah Tourist & Publicity Council.
(Before my resignation in the mid-1960s, this had been
renamed the Utah Travel Council.) Jim was intrigued by
my obvious enthusiasm for Utah and impressed by my Utah
collection.

The T&P Council was a tiny agency with a miniscule
budget and staff; it consisted, as a matter of fact, only
of Jim Cannon, Billie Van Pelt the secretary-administrative
assistant, and several clerical workers as needed. J.
Bracken Lee, Governor Clyde's predecessor, apparently had
not been enthusiastic about the actual or potential role
of tourism in the state's economy. Jim Cannon and the new
governor, George Dewey Clyde - for whom Jim had been campaign manager - saw this role with more optimistic eyes.
The Council's legacy of in-print publications from the Lee
era, to be charitable, was modest.

At that time Jim did not have sufficient budget to hire
me at the Council, even on a part-time basis. But he did
have a few hundred dollars set aside for a complete revision of *Facts About Utah*, a basic publication of the Council.
He assigned it to me on a freelance basis, and I completed
that task during the final two months of 1957.

The book was hardly more than a hundred pages in length,
but that little volume saw five printings and 25,000 copies
before a Council decision to cease publication some years
later. Its compilation was another valuable education in
research, design and publication. Even moreso, it was a
foundation for the in-depth study of Utah's manifold
aspects.

*Facts About Utah* was a digest of the state's geography,
natural and human history, economy, culture, government,
and recreational assets. I gathered details from many
sources, paraphrasing freely from my Utah bible, the old
*Utah: A Guide to the State*. *Facts* was the first of the
books, booklets, brochures, folders, flyers, press releases,
and other published items which I prepared (most of them
without name accreditation) for the Council between 1957
and 1965. I once calculated that they numbered more than a
hundred different items totaling well over a thousand
pages and millions of copies.

Eventually the Council's budget permitted my employment on a part-time, then full-time basis. Jim Cannon became my professional mentor. I idolized and idealized him. He was the first person who ever recognized my Utah interests and talents for whatever worth they had.

Jim was my opposite in public personality. He was gregarious and outgoing almost to an extreme, whereas I was retiring and reserved. Over the years he offered countless opportunities that helped to draw me out socially, but he hardly ever forced them on me. I tried to be a useful right hand.

Having no aspirations for political exposure myself, I walked in Jim's public shadow. Nevertheless, I was not happy with the anonymity accompanying so much of my work. My salary never was more than minimal; it was not adequate compensation for what I did, or so I believed, and name recognition would have helped. Whatever professional recognition I gained eventually was a result more of outside activities than of my Travel Council accomplishments.

Whatever the drawbacks, I cannot imagine a more rewarding seven-plus years than those I spent with the Utah Travel Council. Jim gave me general guidelines, then left me pretty much to my own devices. He was generous in accepting many of my suggestions, though he knew how to pull the reins, particularly when money was involved.

Had Jim Cannon become governor of Utah or mayor of Salt Lake City, as he tried to be in later years, I am certain that governmental budgets and programs would have differed from what fate decreed. He controlled our agency budget with a determination and caution his Scottish ancestors would have admired. The spending of every dollar was calculated on the scale of effective return.

Since he left the Council 20 years ago, millions of dollars have been spent by state, regional, local and commercial interests in Utah, in the attempt to build tourist and recreational travel. My conviction is that much of this has been wasted because of uncoordinated, often ineffective, duplicative, undirected, unimaginative, or otherwise inefficient and wasteful advertising and promotion. With regard to travel promotion and development, my belief is that Utah remains a follower, not a leader or innovator.

That is not to claim that every dollar spent for advertising or promotion is squandered. What I stress is inefficient expenditure. Has a study ever been conducted as to costs versus benefits, potential results versus actual results of promotional expenditures? Have techniques been adapted to coincide with advances in technology and with changing travel trends? I believe not. Other questions need answering as well.

My job with the Council involved research, writing, preparation of publications, public and agency relations, photography, and anything else an "Assistant Director" might be required to do. Duties were varied enough that I rarely became bored until the last year or two. There were always new publications to be created, old ones to be revised, studies and reports to be compiled, letters to be written, pictures to be taken, errands to be run, travel shows and conferences to arrange and attend.

Certainly there was repetition, and psychological ruts were very evident toward the end of my tenure. Still, the very nature of the subject with which I dealt tended continually to challenge my interests and abilities. That subject, of course, was the State of Utah in all its manifestations: a **State** ... a geographical, historical, cultural **Place** ... a dynamic, changing, expanding **Concept** ... a multifaceted **Community** and **Society.**

If Utah had been a place of lesser topographic, historic, economic, and cultural diversity, seven years would have become a torment long before their expiration. Even at that, I must confess that my creative juices had slowed their flow before I resigned in 1965.

Although the basic subject was just as intriguing as ever, perspective and interest priorities had changed. Also, oft-repeated words no longer sufficed to express my feelings. Adjectives, my overworked literary tools, repulsed me with their inadequacy and falseness. Not being adept at metaphor, simile and verse, which might have varied and enlivened my expression, I floundered and moped. I felt like a squeezed-dry sponge.

A psychologist once suggested that perhaps the reason I had such a difficult time writing was that I felt so deeply about Utah I couldn't possibly express my emotions in words - hence my psychological block. He was probably right. Actually, I suppose, I was graduating from the stage of advertising, promotion and mere information-peddling. Years passed, however, before I was able to modify the flamboyant writing habits of those promotional years.

The Travel Council years also were a period of discovering Utah by camera. I had used my first camera as a teen-

ager and took many pictures during the war with a little
35mm Univex. My first serious camera was an Exakta, purchased in 1959. Within the first few months I shot 700
slides with that camera. The Council also had a 4x5 Speed
Graphic which I learned to use.

Jim budgeted very little money for photographs, a
peculiarity of thrift I never did understand. We begged
and borrowed from any source available, to the point of
embarrassment. When it was impossible to obtain photos
otherwise, we paid minimum prices. My job and outside
activities required extensive travel, so Jim agree to provide the film if I would take two shots of every promising
scene, giving one to the Council and keeping the other for
myself. Eventually both the Council and I amassed thousands of my slides. Many of those were used in Council
publications and my own commercial works.

During those years I traveled throughout the state by
car, bus, plane, jeep, and boat. Also I hiked to an extent.
I did not visit every nook and cranny in the state then,
and have not done so yet, and never will. Much better legs
than I possess, plus a helicopter, a four-wheel-drive
vehicle, a boat, horses, and years of additional stamina
would be necessary for that.

It is tiring just to think of the thousands of miles
of canyon bottoms and rims and trails I have not hiked,
the thousands of miles of roads I have not driven, the
mountains I have not climbed, the hundreds of miles of
rivers I have not boated.

Jim took me with him on flights aboard the state plane.
Those flights, together with others I arranged while
filming the state for my own purposes, gave me a good
bird's-eye perspective of Utah's unbelievable topography.

They also solidified my conviction that Utah - at least
with respect to diversity and uniqueness of landscape - is
truly an **Incredible Land.** That conviction I have attempted
to justify in my works over the years.

> *I love Utah.... I am enchanted by it. To me,
> natural Utah is a miracle. It is incredible.*

> Utah the Incredible Land (1965)

At times my sense of wonder at Utah's landscape was
actually painful. I was animated by a flowering appreciation of beauty influenced by religious mysticism. In 1962,
for instance, I wrote the following after a three-day trip:

The Fins in Land of Standing Rocks, Maze District, Canyonlands National Park (above). Warner Lake, La Sal Mountains (below).

"The Needles and Salt Creek country seemed even more inconceivably wonderful to me this time than ever before. . . . Everything down there seemed so perfect to me - so compatible, so ideal - well, so 'perfect' in the ultimate sense of the word. Dead Horse Point was so beautiful it hurt me to look at the view, and I couldn't spend much time at the rim. I just couldn't find adequate words to describe it to myself, and my feelings were almost painful. The LaSals, too, impress me almost painfully with their loveliness of form. I see so much beauty all around me in nature that I am in somewhat of a state of ecstasy whenever I get out into the mountains and deserts."

There were so many trips I cannot even recall more than a few. As an example, I spent five days with Ken Sleight, hiking the Escalante canyons. Several times, with brothers and friends, I probed Robbers Roost, the Hatch canyons of the lower Dirty Devil, and the Standing Rocks in jeeps. With Al Morton and others I participated twice in the Friendship Cruise between Green River and Moab.

There were many trips to western Utah: along the Old Pony Express route; through the Sevier and Escalante deserts; across the salt flats in balloon-tired jeeps; to Stansbury Island; to Antelope Island via the south causeway, north causeway, and by flat-bottomed boat from Fremont Island. I boated Lake Powell and Flaming Gorge Reservoir.

I became acquainted with the Wilcox family of Range Valley, that tremendous tributary of lower Desolation Canyon. The remarkable Wilcox clan consisted of Budge and Pearl with sons Don and Waldo, their wives Jeanette and Julie, and younger children.

Jointly, then separately, the Wilcoxes operated two working cattle ranches on West Tavaputs Plateau, one in Range Valley and another high atop the plateau overlooking Desolation Canyon. Both ranches had facilities for guests. I regarded the Wilcoxes as romantic representatives of Utah's cowboy frontier: proud, self-sufficient, hardworking, enterprising, the prototypes of western individualism. And their ranch settings were out-of-this-world spectacular!

One spring I photographed a Wilcox cattle drive at the old Florence Creek Ranch, Pearl's girlhood home. The cattle were driven to the bank of Green River. There the newborn calves were separated from their mothers; their legs were tied and they were ferried in rubber rafts to

Scenes in the Tavaputs Plateau:  Looking into Desolation
Canyon from Wilcox upper ranch.  Here the canyon is 5,000
feet deep.  (Photo at top.)  The canyon at river level
appears in photo below.

the opposite shore.  Older cattle swam across, and the herd
then was driven to the high country.  I never witnessed a
more interesting or picturesque cattle operation.

There were many other delightful discovery excursions.
The novice, unfamiliar with all that incredible variety
that Utah offers in the way of natural spectacle must
wonder at my enthusiasm; and certainly not everybody,
under the same circumstances, would enjoy what I enjoyed
or react as I did.

Regardless, I was thrilled with my personal discovery
of the haunting Paria country: old Paria ghost town, Cottonwood Canyon, Grosvenor Arch (so exquisite), the East
Kaibab Monocline (Cockscomb), Kodachrome Basin with its
fantastic erotic emblems.

Even the names are interesting: Onion Creek Canyon,
Fisher Towers and Fisher Valley ... Goblin Valley ... the
Dinosaur canyons and Flaming Gorge ... Uinta Basin ...
Willard Mountain and Bountiful Peak ... Stansbury Range
... Pavant Valley ... the Kolob Terrace ... Toroweap ...
Strawberry Point and the Markagunt Plateau ... the Tushars,
Pavant, Paunsaugunt, Sevier, Wasatch, Aquarius, Fish Lake
(nearly all those marvelous High Plateaus, in fact) ...
Skyline Drive ... Nine-Mile Canyon ... Paradox Valley ...
Aneth ... Cedar Breaks ... Kolob canyons ... Mountain
Meadows ... Pine Valley ... Snow Canyon.

I named southern Utah the Lovely, Lonely Land.

The High Plateaus were a special thrill.  How I came to
love them!  Delightful highlands in every way.  Vistas to
burst the heart.  Wooded flanks that explode into rocky
rainbows.  Gentle mountains that transform without warning
into slickrock slopes, bottomless gorges, breathtaking
precipices, amphitheaters filled to the brim with erosional fantasies beyond belief.

Those High Plateaus vistas could transport me to strato-
spheric heights of rapture, as evidenced by my sentimental
Song of the Kolob, written years ago on a Markagunt overlook:

Far to the south the wonderful canyons of the Kolob,
their outlines dim and mysterious in the gentle haze,
softly whisper their song of eternity, of time without
end or beginning.  "Come", they seem to call.  "Come
and let us teach you of God.  Come, and let us show
you how He works.  Let us show you His love of beauty,
His concept of magnificence, the infinite patience in

Bryce Canyon National Park.

Temples of Zion National Park from Kolob road (above).

Castle Rock, Priest and Nuns, Castle Valley.

His labor of creation. Let us show you the pettiness
of moral life, the puniness of man. Come and pray
here in our cloistered depths; come and pray, humbly,
for understanding of the ways of God."

Every time I went on exploring expeditions with my
camera, more often alone than not, I experienced ecstasy
over new discoveries in visual pheomena. No matter how
many times I had seen a place, it was ever new and different, presenting a changed facade each time.

I learned that Utah's landscape is just too intricately
diversified - not only physically but with respect to
changing conditions of perception - ever to be assimilated
and appreciated fully in one lifetime.

Autumn foliage gave me particular delight, so exquisite
I could not bear it at times. "Aspen - their color and
form - almost make me shudder with delight (colored aspen,
that is - or even barren aspen against a blue sky)."

> Golden days - so precious few and brief
>     it seems.
> Saddening as they close, and leaving
>     painful ecstasy
> As perfect Beauty wanes.

My ideas of composition and the beautiful changed during the 1960s. Early in the decade I had evolved from the
appreciation of broad landscapes and big clouds to smaller
things: to individual forms, silhouettes, branches against
the sky, striking trees or clusters of trees, flowers and
closeups.

Oh, those were years of exciting discovery! New people,
new places, new concepts, new facts, new examples of
natural beauty and wonder. An entire world to explore
and experience.

Utah was changing before my eyes, swiftly and profoundly.
The population was growing rapidly, new industries were
being established, city skylines were evolving dramatically. Great dams and artificial lakes came into being, and
the freeway system. The economy was dynamic, optimism
was the spirit of the day.

Renewal and replacement were popular themes, and the Old
disappeared with sickening rapidity - even the priceless,
irreplaceable Old, discarded or replaced with little or no
questioning. During those tragic if dynamic years of the
1950s and 1960s Utah lost a large part of its 19th century

heritage: scores of distinctive mansions, commercial buildings, and religious edifices, as well as countless humbler
structures built of logs, adobe, stone and frame. The
preservation awakening came also, not quite too late to
preserve at least some of the state's architectural keep-
sakes.

I looked at myself as an actor on that stage with a
definite role to play. The Council considered tourism to
be an important growth industry, one of the four or five
key pillars of Utah's economy.

It was Jim Cannon's policy to involve the grass-roots
travel sector in active participation in the building of
tourism, and he attempted to maintain enthusiasm through
personal contact with individuals throughout the state.
The Council sponsored annual travel institutes and the
first Utah Travel Show. We also helped to found Utahns
Inc., a travel-related membership organization that
remained active for some years during the 1960s. Since
then, it seems to me, there has been a weakening of state-
local ties, as the state has assumed a more monolithic
role in travel promotion with marked emphasis on supporting the winter sports industry.

Did I ever question the appropriateness and honesty of
my promotional work? Yes, I did. Often I wondered, "Are
your efforts contributing to eventual degradation of the
very attributes you praise and admire?" How could I deny
that they might?

My rationale went something like this: I was only
indirectly involved in industrial and economic promotion,
so increased population with its attendant negative
results was not exactly my responsibility. Anyway, Utahns
were educated and intelligent. Present them with a problem and they would find a satisfactory solution.

Insofar as tourism was concerned, I believed that
industry was the cleanest and most desirable of industries
if managed wisely. Sightseers took nothing from the land
but memories, and they left dollars behind. I was inord-
inately proud of Utah and wanted everybody else to share
what it had to offer.

That was the good old booster rationale, of course,
which ignored potential regrets of the long-range in favor
of short-term advantages. It is today's booster rationale
of chambers of commerce, state-regional development and
travel agencies. I could not engage in shotgun-type promotion today, at least in good conscience.

However, I still believe that tourism is a desirable industry in respects, admitting at the same time that it can be accompanied by serious environmental problems, is notorious for paying low wages, and is not likely to be the economic panacea so often envisioned for much of the state.

Perhaps my main contribution at the Travel Council was in the field of publications. None of those remain in print. The very nature of Travel Council activity demands constant and frequent revision and replacement. In government, change is always looked upon as progress and improvement, whether or not it is in fact. How can new personnel justify their employment without changing programs?

Times and circumstances do change, of course, and I have no grounds for complaint. I had my hour in the sun. It was my fortune to promulgate significant concepts - some of them new or different ways of viewing the Different World of Utah: its unique landscape, its unusual history, the interesting culture that displays so many admirable and enviable traits.

Inasmuch as my state job paid so little, Jim did not protest when I engaged in outside commercial activities that supplemented and complemented those of the Council but did not represent a conflict of interest or compete with other commercial enterprises.

Schools were in dire need of contemporary Utah study materials. So pressing was this need that schools purchased thousands of the little *Facts About Utah* handbook for classroom use. In 1959 I interviewed teachers and administrators, and on the basis of their expressed interest I compiled a packet of maps, graphs, charts and descriptive text entitled *Materials for the Study of Utah*. School districts purchased 5,000 copies the first year.

Later I modified this unbound packet into ringbound book form, issuing it in various revisions through the early 1970s. By that time it consisted of 94 pages and bore the title *Utah's Geography and Counties*. It was strictly a cottage industry production. Except for the actual printing, Gloria and I did all the gathering, punching, binding and distribution - and, of course, the selling - with occasional hired help. These books were popular with schools, filling a void before the elaborate *Atlas of Utah* appeared.

For years during the 1950s - even before meeting Jim Cannon - I had envisioned a colored pictorial on Utah, the most beautiful publication of its kind. After starting at the Travel Council I continued to think about such a publication, which offered the prospect of longed-for independence. By early 1960 I had settled on the name *Utah Trails* and the format: 48 pages in 8½x11 page size.

I approached Lorin Wheelwright of Wheelwright Lithographing Company, which had the reputation of doing the finest color printing in the state. Lorin was interested. He had Goff Dowding, the firm's art director, make a dummy for my use; and during my few days of vacation in February I traveled up and down the main highways, taking orders from motels and other tourist outlets. In only seven days I obtained pledges for 4,000 copies. Those were not as many as Lorin would have liked, but eventually we made an agreement and began work on Volume I. I did the rough layout, writing, maps, and photo selection. Goff did the finished layout and art.

We received numerous compliments on Volume I and two succeeding volumes in the *Utah Trails* series, which eventually totaled more than 100,000 copies and were still in print a few years ago. Strange to say, however, I never received much financial reward from those books - at least not enough to pay for my time and out-of-pocket expenses. Our profit margin was low and printing costs had repayment priority. The responsibility for sales was a continuing nightmare for me.

Sales volume never did reach the heights I hoped for. Real success was contingent on tourists seeing the books in their rooms and liking them so much they would buy a copy at the desk. This might have worked had it not been for the light-finger proclivities of some motel guests and the unwillingness of motel operators to participate if there were any losses. I believed they should contribute their bit to travel promotion by providing informational literature in their rooms. They did not see it that way, if there was a net cost to them.

. . . In 1965 I ended my employment with the Utah Travel Council. Jim Cannon had not been successful in his 1964 primary bid as Republican nominee for governor. Calvin Rampton, the successful candidate, was a Democrat, so Jim had no chance of retaining his job. E. A. "Manny" Floor, our former account executive with David W. Evans Agency, became the new director with a four- or five-fold increase in budget. Manny and I got along, on the surface at least, and perhaps he would have kept me as Information Director. I do not know. Manny went on to much bigger things after he left the Travel Council.

I was unhappy and burned out. One reason was overwork: for example, I put in 60 hours of overtime in June alone, working on 13 different publications, eight of them at the same time. Also, Manny was a human dynamo, a frenetic worker whose vibes did not coincide with mine.

Most importantly, the glamor had gone. The big budget increase took away the challenges Jim and Billie and I had met in stretching our meager funds as far as they would go. Now the challenge would be in trying to spend a million dollars in two years without wasting it.

## ON MY OWN

Having, as so many times before and since, the desire for self-sufficiency, I resigned in August of 1965. I had purchased a Bolex 16mm movie camera a few months earlier and planned to create an "art" film on Utah to be entitled *The Varied Face of Utah: An Adventure in Beauty.* I believed then that people would appreciate a film on natural beauty if it was dramatic enough. Now I am not so sure. I hoped to use it for lecture purposes.

Also, my new guidebook *Utah the Incredible Land* had recently been published by Wheelwright. Some 10,000 copies of that book and 18,000 copies of the pictorial were stacked frighteningly high, waiting for me to sell them. Prospects were good for freelance writing, sale of photos and school materials, preparation of geography films for schools, etc. Somehow I would make it.

Ah, what faith! But I was not completely unsuccessful, as time would tell. For many years, with the exception of one part-time job, Gloria and I did manage to survive on the basis of our own ingenuity.

That year of 1965 also saw a boating trip to the Sea of Cortez, and a trip to the World's Fair in New York City.

My movie camera opened photographic windows I had never looked through. With its long zoom lens and adjustable shutter speeds, the Bolex was more versatile than my 35mm camera. I used it to shoot everything that caught my fancy: flowers, insects, moving clouds, people, animals, static scenery, aerials, rock designs, fluttering leaves, abstracts of all kinds. I could tilt, pan, zoom, speed movement and slow it down.

Water especially intrigued me. Water moved, creating endless changing designs in the process. Reflections were fascinating. I photographed seeps, springs, lakes, mountain creeks and desert rivers, waterfalls, dramatic flash floods, exotic mud and sand patterns, wave designs of Great Salt Lake from the air. Aerials of the red-rock terrain were wonderful to the point of incredibility.

By the end of 1965 I had enough 16mm film footage to edit three films: two films on Utah's geography for schools and one lecture film. Interviews with educators had encouraged me that enough orders would be forthcoming to cover my costs and give me some profit. (At that time schools were receiving federal funds for instructional materials they could not otherwise afford.) During the winter and following spring I edited all three films.

Being a rank amateur at film editing, final results were not exactly polished products. "It's a horrible job of gleaning scenes from 50 or 60 rolls of film, hanging them on nails, making up an outline for the script, arranging the scenes, cutting them to the right lengths and then splicing together. For a 40-minute show this means I handle perhaps 400 different or separate scenes." That is what I wrote concerning the lecture film.

For each of the geography films a refined and timed script was required, to which the film must be matched down to the second as measured by film footage. Fades and dissolves necessitated overlapping A and B reels, and the sound tape had to be correlated laboriously with the film footage. Then everything was sent to the film lab in Hollywood for answer prints, which finally arrived after several weeks of anxious waiting.

All this was a bit overwhelming for my untrained abilities. "All the time, of course, I'm stewing and wondering whether my scenes are the right length and whether they'll tell the story I want to tell; above all is the black cloud of doubt: will it bore people, inspire them as I want it to, or just leave them apathetic?"

School districts purchased 23 prints of my two geography films, one on the Colorado Plateau and one on the Rocky Mountains and Great Basin. There were technical flaws, but under the circumstances of limited market, I believe the schools got their money's worth. Though I was not really proud of those films in a professional way, I made little profit and could not afford to invest more money in perfecting them. Besides, the schools had no funds to buy additional prints.

. . . The year 1966 was a bright landmark in my life, and not with respect to career. I asked Gloria to marry me, she accepted, and we were married in June.

When Gloria became my companion, I became We. No longer was I lonely. I had no more deep depressions. Her vibrancy, happiness, and sheer joie-de-vivre have always buoyed sagging spirits before they could plunge to previous depths. Even now, 20 years later, I cannot believe such love, support and acceptance. Gloria sees the beauties I see, and we share in common not only the physical things of our lives but most of the intangible as well. Such a relationship of perfect compatibility is more than I ever hoped was possible.

Gloria and I had known each other for several years before our marriage, so we were aware of each other's eccentricities. She had had a stressful life and had worked on Broadway as a saleslady for some years. Charm and grace were among the attributes I treasured in Gloria; also her enthusiasm for nature and art of all kinds, and her love for people. With equanimity and devotion she accepted the serious problem of my invalid mother, who depended upon us for assistance.

Gloria and I helped to nurse my mother until her death in 1971, vowing to keep her at home with us, then in my brother's house next to ours. Only intermittently were hospitals and nursing homes necessary, and for that we were profoundly grateful. My mother Alta was a selfless matriarch to whom all our family owed more than we could ever repay.

Not long after our marriage we applied to the Small Business Administration for a loan of several thousand dollars to revise my films and school textbook, and also to produce a series of filmstrips, maps and display prints. The loan was approved, and during the summer and fall of 1967 I worked on those projects.

The filmstrips required copying of hundreds of historic photos at the Historical Society as well as creation of numerous maps, charts, titles, etc., which I prepared. Eight filmstrips were completed that year and twelve the following year, all together containing about a thousand separate frames. Each strip was accompanied by a recorded tape.

Schools continued to purchase those filmstrips for many years, despite what was to me a catastrophic cutoff of federal aid in 1969. They preserved our solvency more than once.

The author with some of his published works on Utah.   1966.

Sipapu Bridge, Natural Bridges National Monument.

## Part Three

# ENLIGHTENMENT:
# THE ENCHANTED WILDERNESS

### WIDENING HORIZONS: THE COLORADO PLATEAU

It was in 1967 that I was inspired to make a knock-'em-dead lecture film on the Colorado Plateau - not just Utah's part of the Plateau but the great region-wide Colorado Plateau.

I knew, of course, that Utah's borders contained much of the choicest scenery on the Plateau, included in Canyonlands and the High Plateaus. However, that part of the Plateau in Arizona, Colorado and New Mexico was spectacular as well, besides being geologically fascinating. Aspects of geology, apart from scenery, were just then beginning to attract my attention.

With Gloria or by myself, that summer and fall, I filmed in all four states, on the ground, from the air, and on Lake Powell. During the winter of 1967-68 I edited my footage into a 70-minute film which I entitled *The Enchanted Wilderness: A film portrait of the world's most amazing region, the great Colorado Plateau of the West.*

Exactly when the term Enchanted Wilderness came to mind I cannot say, other than it originated during that winter. The film was completed by April 1968 and I showed it to Sierra Club staffers in San Francisco in June. That summer I tried to get on a western lecture circuit, and in November Gloria and I showed the film to an audience in Kingsbury Hall.

During that same period I completed three triple-image slide shows, a glass-mounted series entitled *Adventures in Beauty.* Each show contained about 500 slides, projected two or three at a time.

I found no paying market for either the lecture film or slide shows. Those who saw my productions were complimentary, or many of them were, and probably I could have kept busy projecting my shows free of charge, at least in

Utah. Perhaps I could have made a little money on the west coast, where the population was many times greater.

I really do regret the ending to that episode, not as much because of financial loss and discouragement as because we did have something very beautiful to offer people but could not do so because of various frustrations. Did I persevere sufficiently? Would I have succeeded eventually or was the lecture concept basically unrealistic? Who can know? Experience supports the negative view.

Years later I put together another two-part film on the Colorado Plateau, directed toward earth science students in high school and college. Two reels made the film too long for classroom use, so I condensed the film to a 26-minute one-reeler, printed an attractive advertising folder, and circularized hundreds of prospective users. The market for sales, I found, did not exist.

These multiple projects were not all failures in every way. They certainly were educational for us. I do not regret them except in the sense of hurt, and even hurt can be worthwhile as an obstacle to overcome and discard.

## BIRTH OF A CONCEPT

Those joyful days and months of filming the Colorado Plateau during the late 1960s - traversing it from end to end and side to side, in all kinds of weather and every season, on the ground and in the air - were among the most ecstatic of my life. And dear Gloria was with me part of the time, sharing my joy and amplifying it with hers.

We learned to appreciate more than ever how truly miraculous that region is, geologically and esthetically. Our realization of the Enchanted Wilderness concept expanded, solidified and took more definite form. We came to believe that we had a special vision shared by pitifully few others.

Never before, so far as I am aware, had the Plateau been visualized in its entirety as an **"Enchanted Wilderness"**.

As ordinarily thought of, the wilderness concept is confined to pristine territory that has not been developed with structures, established roads, mines, etc. In that restrictive sense the Colorado Plateau certainly does not qualify **in total** as wilderness. It contains numerous cities and towns (most of them small), thousands of miles of roads (the great majority of them unpaved), countless mine shafts and excavation scars, dams, reservoirs, fences,

**Telluride** in the San Juan Mountains, Colorado, an Enchanted Wilderness border area (above). Monument Valley, Utah-Arizona, looking west from Comb Ridge and Chinle Wash on the Navajo Indian Reservation (below).

and other works of mankind--not to mention overgrazing abuses by livestock, timber cuts, and so on.

Nevertheless, **relatively speaking** and considering it as a distinctive, integral region with fairly well-defined boundaries, the Colorado Plateau surely is one of the largest **relatively undeveloped** parts of the 48 contiguous states. Millions of acres are completely uninhabited. Where roads do exist in some of those areas, they are likely to be fair-weather vehicle trails. Its total population numbers only several hundred thousand, mostly in small towns or a few modest cities, while large urban areas are a hundred miles or more away from the Plateau's boundaries.

The great majority of the region's land is owned by federal-state governments or by Indian tribes; is almost wholly unsuitable for profitable agriculture (because of ruggedness, lack of usable water, etc.); and contains few marketable minerals of strategic scarcity. At the same time its landscape is exceptionally scenic, having a strange, dramatic, marvelous beauty found in few other places on earth. Parts of this landscape are completely unique.

As for its being "enchanted", that of course is a personal evaluation. Gloria and I consider it as "enchanted" as a region could be, and we are not alone in that opinion. If New Mexico - which contains the least-distinctive part of the Plateau - merits the appellation "Land of Enchantment" (and who could argue?), then the entire Plateau certainly qualifies as an enchanted land.

However justified, between 1968 and 1973 we applied the name Enchanted Wilderness to films, tour brochures, an association, a magazine, bulletins, travel show exhibit, media ads, and other printed materials.

For the region's very salvation, we believe with our hearts, the region should be thought of as an Enchanted Wilderness by every person who appreciates its uniqueness and cares about its ultimate destiny.

This way of looking at the Colorado Plateau did not occur full-bloom. It was no spontaneous revelation. It grew as familiarity with the region expanded. I suppose it was the evolutionary result of nearly 30 years of exploratory probings and study.

While Utah had been the focus of my travels and creative work, I certainly was aware that the Colorado Plateau was not confined to that state. Circumstances, however,

had not developed much on-site acquaintance with the
Plateau outside of Utah before 1967, when I filmed in
Arizona, Colorado and New Mexico.

That summer and fall I filmed the Mogollon Rim and the
San Francisco volcanic zone near Flagstaff. I also char-
tered a plane to fly over the Oak Creek Canyon breaks,
which are incredibly beautiful from the air - moreso even
than from the ground. I visited the Zuni country, El
Morro, the Hopi mesas, Shiprock, seeing more of the Navajo
and Four Corners country than ever before. I filmed Mesa
Verde, the San Juan Mountains, Grand Mesa, Black Canyon
of the Gunnison, Grand River Valley, Colorado National
Monument, and White River country.

Autumn foliage that year was glorious, especially on
Grand Mesa and in the San Juan Mountains near Ridgway
and Ouray. I fell in love with western Colorado then and
have returned many times with Gloria, to Ouray, Silver-
ton, Durango, Mesa Verde and other places. Next to Utah,
that part of the United States is dearest to our hearts.

## SCHOOL OF THE EARTH

Being a teacher by training and inclination, quite
naturally I came to consider the educational potential of
the Colorado Plateau.

Knowledgeable geologists, of course, have long been
aware that the Colorado Plateau is probably the world's
most comprehensive exhibit of geologic processes concentrated in a single compact region and exposed to easy
observation. Considered as an integrated topographic area,
it appears to have no counterpart in the world for variety
of structural and erosional forms, rock types, and ecological terrain. Even the Plateau's range of vegetative
and animal types is remarkable. Bonuses for visitors are
the Plateau's intriguing cultures (past and present),
abundant minerals, fossil deposits, rivers and lakes, and
so on.

In 1968 and 1969 Gloria and I investigated the purchase
of property in the small town of Torrey, 60 miles east of
Richfield, 210 miles south of Salt Lake City, and only a
short distance from Capitol Reef National Park. Our
interest was stimulated by our friends Roselyn and Don
Phillips of Tooele, who had purchased a lot in Torrey.

Torrey is on a frontier of sorts, being situated in a
valley of rainbow cliffs on the western margin of the

Poncho House Ruin, Navajo Indian Reservation. Josef Muench, photographer, stands atop the cliff as an inconspicuous dot.

Cliff Palace Ruin, Mesa Verde National Park (above). Literally
thousands of prehistoric structures and rock art sites attest
to ancient cultures that once inhabited the Enchanted Wilderness.
Green River Canyon from North Point (below).

Canyonlands region. Thousand Lake Mountain and Boulder
Mountain/Aquarius Plateau, components of the High Plateaus
region, loom to north and south respectively. Five other
modest towns and hamlets are nearby to the west, but only
a few hundred people in half a dozen small settlements
inhabit the entire vast, empty semi-wilderness between
Torrey and Blanding-Green River, the nearest towns of any
size to the east. These are 175 and 100 miles away.

I describe our Torrey years in Part Four. Suffice to
say here that Torrey epitomized the red-rock country for
us. It was surrounded by the most gorgeous earth colors
imaginable and erosional designs of such wonder and
exquisiteness that just looking at them could make a person weak. The town itself was a model of pioneer rusticity.
There were mountains, forests, lakes and rivers within an
hour's drive or less, and the red-rock wilderness began
just east of town.

So we bought a 1.6-acre lot in 1969 and planned to begin
a new life as soon as conditions favored such a move.

Seven years passed before we made that move. In the
meantime we traveled the 210 miles from Salt Lake City
times without number, cleaning out the log cabin shell on
our lot, planning how we would restore it as a suitable
place for casual living.

In the fall of 1969 I woke up in the hours before dawn
with a new idea crystallized in my mind. It was the strong
conviction that geology tours of the Colorado Plateau
would be a successful business endeavor. And Torrey could
be a base, a campus as it were, for such a School of the
Earth.

For many years, I knew, schools had sent students to
the Plateau for geological field work. However, much more
could be done in the way of bringing not only students but
the general public to the Plateau for study of the earth.
Or so I thought. For non-specialists, greater stress could
be placed on scenic aspects than on technical factors. I
reasoned that education could be combined with esthetic
and recreational pleasure. People surely would jump at
such an unusual offering.

The impetus from that pre-dawn vision was so powerful
that within a few weeks I had conveyed my enthusiasm to a
group of eminent teachers of geology at University of
Utah, Southern Utah State College, and Weber State College.
Before the year was out we had organized Natural History
Inc. and were renting downtown office space. Our mission:

Educational Tours and Directed Field Study in the Enchanted
Wilderness of the Colorado Plateau and Its Borderlands.

Eventually our board of directors included a professor
of history, an attorney, a professor of English, a river
tour operator, and a number of geology teachers. All
directors were investors, and I was executive director.

Basically our company planned to do advertising and
attend to travel logistics, relying on professional guides
and commercial firms for transportation. Members of the
board could be tour leaders or arrange for such from college faculties.

Ours was an idealistic and logical concept. Education
was booming in every field and among every age group, and
Arthur C. Clarke had prophesied that education would be
the biggest activity of mankind by the end of the century. The overseas student travel industry was at its
height; also the commercial tour industry of Canyonlands
was flourishing as numerous operators conveyed thousands
of visitors into the area's remotest reaches by bus,
jeep, boat, raft, plane, afoot or on horseback.

NHI's budget was not lush but it did provide funds for
an attractive brochure and tour literature, a modest
amount of media advertising, and direct promotional mailings to 5,000 university teachers.

All of us were hopeful and enthusiastic during the
early months of 1970. Probably I had never been happier
than I was the night it was decided to incorporate.
Optimism and faith kept us afloat during three traumatic
years.

By June it was evident we would have no tour season
in 1970. The country was entering a recession, and though
our advertising brought hundreds of inquiries there were
few solid bookings. It was necessary to cancel even those
when it became apparent that groups would not be large
enough to justify the costs of running tours.

That summer, for Gloria and me, was an economic depression, as were the following three years. I was not drawing enough salary from the company to pay our bills;
Gloria's income from her job was pitifully low; cutoff of
federal funding had decimated my school business and was
destroying other audiovisual businesses. And so on.

"But to counteract all these worries," I wrote then,
"ordinarily enough to drive me insane, I have the serenity
of my religious faith and my mission and the belief in

eventual triumph. And my wonderful little exuberant
Gloria, without whose gladness I'd be very morose indeed.
And our pretty little home, so cute now with new paint.
And the love for and by my mother and family; my work,
beauty - and hope, hope, hope."

## THE ENCHANTED WILDERNESS ASSOCIATION

"Eventual triumph" never did come in the form of success for NHI or its offspring, the Enchanted Wilderness
Association. Before they succumbed in 1973, Gloria and I
were forced to sell our pretty little home, mother had
died, Gloria had quit her job to help me in the office,
and the two of us were left with thousands of dollars in
organization debts to pay off by ourselves.

After the disappointing first season, NHI's directors
agreed to keep the organization alive. Some of them
invested more money, and they approved my plan to form the
Enchanted Wilderness Association (EWA).

In substance, EWA was conceived first as a division of
NHI, later as a separate non-profit corporation, with the
mission of advertising NHI's tours as well as tours and
services offered by other firms in the region. In effect
it was to be a regional promotion agency engaged in cooperative national advertising.

EWA would publish a magazine containing advertisements;
would do national media advertising; and would distribute
business literature at travel shows or through cooperative mailings. Also, memberships would be solicited from
people interested in the region who might become tour
patrons at some time or other. EWA would also provide
travel planning assistance to members.

On our shoestring budget, those plans were utterly
impossible of realization. That fact is easily seen in
hindsight; but at the time, of course, we were grasping
at any possibility that might offer even a remote chance
of success.

In February 1971 our one and only issue of the *Enchanted
Wilderness Magazine* appeared, too late to be of help in
our display at the Anaheim Travel Show. Gloria was the
magazine's art director, I was editor. With the help of
salesmen we had obtained enough paying ads to cover some
of the printing cost of the magazine's 12,000 copies. However, there was not enough advertising support for a second
issue, nor sufficient funds for all the national advertising we had planned. Our ads did appear in *Natural History*,

*Audubon*, and *Desert* magazines. And NHI did conduct several tours in 1971, proving there was at least a modicum of interest in what it had to offer.

Largely on the basis of EWA's attractive magazine, the association eventually attracted about a thousand members and subscribers, as well as numerous contributors of funds. In lieu of magazines, which we could not afford, we issued six bulletins in 1971 and 1972 as well as other mailings. Trying to keep the faith, however, became impossible. Bulletin No. 6, issued in September 1972, was EWA's last.

. . . What had we ·learned from those traumatic years? Many things, of course.

Above all, we learned that unsuspected multitudes were interested in the Colorado Plateau, its uses and destiny. We received a large number of encouraging letters and monetary contributions. And EWA was just one little organization among many. The Sierra Club, with a vast membership, was concerned with the region. The Wilderness Society, Audubon Society, and Wasatch Mountain Club were actively involved with Plateau issues. So were other groups, not to mention individuals acting independently.

Perhaps most importantly, we learned or suspected the following: The Colorado Plateau as a regional destination, especially in the guise of an "Enchanted Wilderness", was unknown to the traveling public.

We were unprepared pioneers of a new idea in a too-little-known land. Nevertheless, even today, we believe that our basic idea of educational tours in the Plateau is valid, and that we were just ahead of our times.

The Enchanted Wilderness is more than a geographic region, more than an idea. It is a force, an intangible movement. It lies written in the heart of every person who loves the red-rock country, who wants the preservation of wild areas, clean air, a halt to rape of the land for profit. It is a living pulse of today. It touches on our state and bordering states. It reminds us of our past – our mistakes, our regrets, our shame. It is our future, our hope, the eternal gratitude of future generations. So you see, this is more than an idea. You can recognize it. It is ours now: our heritage, the beacon for our understanding, the Enchanted Wilderness.

*Gloria*

*Part Four*

# NEW BEGINNINGS:
# SLEEPING RAINBOW YEARS

Between the end of our Enchanted Wilderness projects in 1972 and our move to the Land of the Sleeping Rainbow in 1976, another dark age of sorts ensued. We tried to sell books by mail and to provide audiovisual materials for schools in the surrounding states. We sold our home for living expenses and to pay company debts. We tried to stir up commercial, governmental and legislative interest in a Utah state magazine.

Jobs for men of my age and generalist experience were nonexistent, or at least I could not find one. Finally, after a year of searching, I obtained a clerk's position at the main postoffice in Salt Lake City. That job was our financial deliverance.

Soon after starting work at the postoffice, I produced - with Goff Dowding's artistic help - one of the most attractive small illustrated publications ever published in Utah. That was Volume 3 of the *Utah Trails* series. I was proud of it, though it did not bear my name.

Also, for a New York publisher, I compiled the manuscript for a social studies textbook on the intermountain states. The extensive research involved in that compilation gave me a much more comprehensive insight into the geography, economy and culture of the Four Corners states and Nevada - a knowledge that only strengthened my conviction of the uniqueness and incalculable worth of the Colorado Plateau as a frontier on which humanity could exercise unprecedented foresight and constraint, or its customary ignorant rapacity.

### TORREY

Whenever possible Gloria and I went to Torrey. During the worrisome months before my postal job saved our financial skins we had sold our Torrey lot and cabin, but in

the meantime – with my brothers – we were making payments
on a more desirable lot two blocks away.

This lot was bordered on two sides by a canal, which
watered an extraordinarily lush growth of cottonwood
trees, alfalfa, rabbitbrush, asparagus, lilacs, and a
multitude of other plants. Occupied at one time, years
before, it was vacant and overgrown when we bought it.
That beautiful lot, or our half of it, was where we planned to build our home and start a new life.

Our Torrey dream did not lose its vividness as my hip
joints deteriorated and the pain increased. Fortunately
my clerical job required little standing or walking, so
with the aid of a dozen aspirin a day I worked for a year
before having both joints replaced in 1974.

That operation was a milestone in my life. Whereas
for years I had been a semi-cripple, now I could walk and
hike and climb and do physical work, all without painful
distress! My body was resurrected. I was a new man.

We purchased a pickup truck and began hauling building
materials to Torrey as they became available at special
prices: useful things we picked up as bargains, such as
doors, cabinets, windows, piping, and electrical components from an old school building that was being demolished.
We ordered rough-cut planking and timbers from a Torrey
lumberman, and arranged with him to build a bridge across
the canal as well as haul some 30-foot logs from the top
of Boulder Mountain. We planted evergreens and semi-
dwarf fruit trees.

One of the first tasks was to clear our building site,
a formidable job in itself because of so much vegetation
and fallen branches which had to be gathered, then burned.
Burning in Torrey is hazardous because of strong breezes
and wind that blow almost constantly. Tinder is so plenti-
ful in the form of dry weeds and brush that an out-of-
control fire, fanned by a wind, could sweep much of the
town in a short time. And because of our carelessness and
ignorance, that almost happened with us one day.

I knew very little about construction, having had no
formal training or much experience even in carpentry. Of
electric wiring and plumbing I was completely ignorant.
We plunged ahead blindly and willfully, but not without
purpose.

Reflecting on those days, Gloria and I often wonder
what motivated us to make that move. Torrey really was

an obsession with me, moreso than with Gloria. What drove us? Income prospects in Torrey certainly were tenuous.

One motive we can identify was retreat from a troublesome environment. I was not happy on my postal job, and in fact its non-challenging routine kept me in emotional turmoil. The Torrey dream gave us something to look forward to: growth in individualism, overcoming new challenges, abandoning old ways, building a new life in new surroundings, away from the urban hassle and scenes of so much disappointment and stress.

Then, of course, my heart (if not Gloria's to the same extent) had always been in the red-rock country, which I had visited countless times but only on frustratingly brief occasions. Finally, after my hip operations, there was the exciting prospect of using my body, almost for the first time, in physical work. I looked forward with intensity to that experience.

Gloria, being as ignorant of future vicissitudes as I, participated willingly and enthusiastically in the plans.

I purchased a small library of how-to books on all aspects of construction. The design of our house came straight out of my head, with Gloria's approval.

We wanted to defy normal design conventions and to incorporate personal preferences, which included overhead spaciousness, overhead windows, walls of irregular height, and openness throughout the house. Above all we wanted to avoid monotonous uniformity in walls and surfaces.

My brother Darrell, a builder, expressed his blunt opinion of our final plans. He said that we could hardly have designed a house that would require more extra time and labor in angled cuts, joints, special lengths, weatherproofing, and so on. He was right. We knew the problems but were willing to face them if the final product was what we wanted.

Basically our home is a five-sided tepee or pyramid with steeply sloping roof-sides of differing dimensions. A sunroom annex protrudes from the southeast side, providing solar heat in winter; a kitchen-bath-utility annex projects from the north side. Both annexes are joined openly to the central tepee, and four of the roof-sides contain windows. The bedroom area is partitioned off from the central tepee area, which rises to an open peak 22 feet above the floor. All together the house contains 1,500 square feet of floor area.

Since our bridge was not strong enough for heavy loads such as a cement truck, we supported the house on posts rather than a concrete foundation. The main tepee superstructure consists of a central pole or log embedded in a 55-gallon drum filled with concrete; this central pole is joined at the top by five 30-foot logs which fan out to support a system of 6-inch beams. Onto these we placed a roof of 2-inch planks, urethane insulation, and cedar shakes. Logs, beams and planks are of rough-cut stump-dried Engelmann spruce from the top of Boulder Mountain. Gloria and I built the entire house ourselves, with the exception of the main power connection and the shake roofing.

We placed our central pole in concrete on Memorial Day in 1976, the Bicentennial Year, naming it our May Pole. In July we made our permanent move. Not being comfortable in our camping van, we sold it and substituted a ramshackle lean-to for Gloria's bed and cooking setup. I placed my cot in a high-sided horse trailer with a tarp stretched overhead. Neither facility kept us dry during summer showers, but we did survive through rain and cold until November. I built a three-sided pit toilet, open to the unpopulated south where Boulder Mountain and the jagged Cockscomb provided magnificent subjects for meditation.

That summer was occupied with installing the water line, building a storage shed, attaching the outrigger logs to the center pole, and then building the kitchen-bath-utility annex. Measuring 16 by 22 feet, that little domicile was our home for several years. We moved in on October 31 and had our Thanksgiving dinner there. A little sheepherder's wood stove kept us warm with frequent stokings through the night.

Next year we added a small bed space to the annex, as work on the main tepee proceeded at a glacial pace. Darrell's prophecy as to the in-built difficulties of our design proved all too accurate, in that many beams had to be accurately angled on at least one end - not an easy task with every beam end requiring four cuts with a small power saw.

Gloria helped as her strength and small size permitted, but juggling and fitting those heavy beams and planks was a torturous job. Some of the longer beams weighed 80 pounds; the outrigger logs were pulled up with the truck, using a cable threaded through a pulley at the top of the center pole.

Construction became my specialty. Gloria did the inter-

Our house in Torrey.

South face of Thousand Lake Mountain and Fremont River
Valley as seen from Donkey Point on Aquarius Plateau.
Torrey and Teasdale are in this valley.

ior painting and decorating, providing those artistic
touches that made our house a home. The rusticity of the
rough wood required decorating genius to make it attractive, and Gloria provided that genius. She helped erect
the interior rock work, designed our aspen mosaics,
decorated the walls, and refinished the furniture. She
kept a vegetable garden, planted a lawn and flowers, added
landscaping touches, and did exterior painting. Most
importantly, she has always kept our spirits up.

Hammering thousands of 16-penny nails by hand, through
2-inch planks, finally injured my shoulder, though fortunately not until most of the heavy nailing was done.
Even more stressful was the necessity for climbing. I
had a severe case of acrophobia; my fear of heights was
extreme. Even an eight-foot roof made me fearful, and
as the scaffold inside the tepee crept higher toward the
22-foot peak, that dread increased. Psychologists are
right with respect to fear: I faced mine (not willingly)
and conquered it, at least partially. Normal roofs no
longer bother me.

Shakes were installed on the tepee three years after we
arrived in Torrey, and we expanded into that spacious
area shortly thereafter, even before the floor was completed. The sunroom required another year or so. We also
built a large workshop-storage building and a storage pit.
My work on *Utah: A Guide to the State* required at least
half of my attention between 1978 and 1982, so even now
the house is not quite finished. Probably it never will be.

Since the tepee was in a skeletal state for years, towns-
people and passersby wondered what kind of monstrosity was
coming up on our lot and when, if ever, it would be completed.

Don and Roselyn Phillips, our friends from Tooele, were
building a house several blocks from ours. Roselyn held a
full-time job at Tooele Army Depot, coming down on weekends
to be with Don, who worked steadily on the house during
warmer months. In his 70s, Don worked relentlessly from
dawn to dusk, year after year. The result was a showplace
which hosted visitors by the score before his death a few
years ago.

Don and Roselyn were our friends in the real sense, providing refreshment, encouragement, interest, and a bath
when needed. They involved us with their visitors, some
of whom became our friends too. Life would not have been
nearly as pleasant without them.

Personal relations were not our prime reason for the
Torrey move, of course.  Both Gloria and I like to read,
drive, and walk.  During the building years we were usually
too tired to miss the human companionship so lacking eight
months of the year.  Now this paucity is more of a problem
for us.  We miss compatible human association, which is
restricted mostly to the summer months, when friends and
family stop by now and then.  We exchange visits then with
summer residents, a number of whom come from California.
With some of them we have a warm relationship.

That is not to say there are no local friends.  There
are.  But Wayne County does not afford a rich social diet
for those who are not church-goers.

We number among our valued friends a few old-timers who
have lived in the county most or all of their lives.
Their parents and grandparents were settlers of the 1880s
and 1890s, real pioneers who came to a harsh, even desolate
frontier.  No part of Utah offered more obstacles to settlement.  In the upper valley the climate was severe with
cold winters and short growing season.  Farther east, the
only favorable sites for settlement were along the few
streams, where water was available but floods were an
ever-present danger and a frequent, fearsome actuality.

None of the original pioneers were alive when we arrived,
but many of their children and grandchildren were.  We
became acquainted with some of these people.  With prompt-
ing they would tell us tales of floods, hunger, heat and
cold, bad roads, near-poverty, poor drinking water, ruined
crops, poignant dramas of birth, death and sickness.

Behind the sad tales, not so often expressed but
implicit, were the joys and happiness of family and community.  There is no denying that existence in early Wayne
County was unusually difficult and that there were relatively few diversions from the humdrum.  So it is not surprising that memory selects for emphasis the traumatic
event, which more often had connotations of sadness than
of gladness.

Torrey was known at one time as Poverty Flat, and its
people generally were not as prosperous as those in older
towns to the west.  Streams flow on either side of the bench
on which the townsite is placed; however, they are at a
level far below the town, requiring culinary and irrigation
water to be brought long distances by ditches and canals.
Until fairly recent decades culinary water came from ditches
into settling cisterns.  Many homes were humble structures; some of these remain.

Farming, stockraising and orchards provided a meager livelihood for a time, but those activities could not support a growing population. Gradually, most young people moved away and the older ones died. By the 1950s and 1960s Torrey was a semi-ghost town. Not all young people joined the out-migration willingly. Wayne natives tend to love their beautiful wild land, but not all can make a living here.

While doing background research for my book *Seeing Capitol Reef National Park*, I read books about Wayne County and interviewed a number of old-timers. They told me stories about the pioneers; and interesting anecdotes about how places such as Whiskey Flat, Whiskey Spring, Ford Hill and Ferns Nipple got their names; and tales of Depression days when people really had to scrounge to put bread on their tables.

So many interesting people have passed through our lives since we came to Torrey! Dean Brimhall was one of them. He had a retreat in Fruita and when we knew him, in the early 1970s, he was elderly and frail but still obsessed with locating, cataloging and photographing ancient Indian petroglyphs and pictographs. Probably nobody knew the location of more Canyonlands rock art sites than Dean, but he was secretive about the choicest, least-known sites and abhorred the brainless vandalism that has damaged so many antiquities.

Since 1960 or thereabouts, when I was with the Travel Council, I had been acquainted with Lurt and Alice Knee. Owners of Sleeping Rainbow guest ranch, 15 or 20 miles south of Fruita, Lurt and Alice provided American-plan accommodations and vehicle tours for select clientele from many states and even foreign countries.

Lurt arrived in this country during the 1930s and fell in love with the old Floral Ranch on Pleasant Creek, established by Ephraim Hanks and his family in the 1880s. He purchased the ranch from Levi and Billie Bullard. Lurt changed the name to Sleeping Rainbow, which he says was a name applied by Navajo Indians to the varicolored Chinle rock formation of Arizona and Utah. With the ranch as a base, he set up a tour operation that gradually gained renown as one of the best of its kind in the Four Corners region.

As Lurt's second wife, Alice joined him in building modern accommodations. Guests ate at a large table in the rustic lodge. Lurt and Alice provided a variety of day

Waterpocket Fold and the white temples of Sheets Gulch,
looking north from Strike Valley Overlook, Capitol Reef
National Park.

Cathedrals in Upper Cathedral Valley, Capitol Reef National Park.

tours to Cathedral Valley, the Circle Cliffs, Boulder
Mountain and Thousand Lake Mountain, the Henry Mountains,
San Rafael Swell, Goblin Valley, and other places. Longer
trips could be arranged to Robbers Roost, Standing Rocks,
the Escalante country, etc.

Lurt came naturally to his occupation, having helped
Harry Goulding, his brother-in-law, establish his trading
post-lodge in Monument Valey. He was also related in
some way to Art Greene, a pioneer of Colorado River-Lake
Powell boating tours and a founder of the Wahweap marina
near Page.

Lurt and Alice probably were more responsible than anybody else in opening up the West Canyonlands region to
tourist travel. Articles appeared in numerous publications
describing their tours and the strange, exotic, wild land
in which they operated. Among many professional photographers they hosted were Josef and David Muench.

The lives of Riley "Jack" and Erma Osborn, older friends
of ours in Torrey, illustrate many of the challenges and
activities of middle-generation Wayne County residents.

Erma, now in her 70s, was born in a log cabin in the
remote wilds southeast of Torrey. Her mother died soon
after Erma's birth, and the infant was left with her two-
year-old brother while their father went for help. Soon
afterwards a passing rider stopped at the cabin, fed and
comforted them until their father returned. A reclusive
prospector, Erma's father left the children with a family
in Torrey. She grew up with this family, who operated a
small hotel or boarding house, and was married to Jack as
a young woman.

Riley "Jack" came to the county from Oklahoma in the
1920s as a geologist-prospector, enticed by the copper and
gold prospects of Miners Mountain. Jack married Erma soon
after he arrived. Over the years he has been a farmer,
miner, deputy sheriff, justice of the peace, and long-time
district ranger with the Fish and Game Department (now
Wildlife Resources).

Jack is now in his mid-90s, still sprightly and active,
keeping a garden, driving his own car. He continues to
maintain mining claims on Miners Mountain and in Tantalus
Basin. Prospects for development or sale have alternated
over the years between promising and discouraging, but
Jack keeps hoping as all true prospectors do.

We also became acquainted with author Pearl Baker, who
spent her girlhood on the Robbers Roost ranch and later

wrote prolifically about Butch Cassidy and the Wild Bunch.
We knew Richard Sprang, creator of the Batman character.
Sprang, with his wife Elizabeth, built a showplace home
in the lovely Fish Creek cove south of Torrey. We came
to know Ralph Lowe, an Ogden attorney who fell in love
with the Torrey Breaks area while flying a plane. He came
back, purchased land, and built the Rimrock Motel-Resort
east of town.

Among our closest friends are summer migrants from
California, Colorado and northern Utah. These are mostly
retired people who have homes in Torrey or Teasdale and
come to spend the summer months as a diversion of sorts,
or to escape the heat. Some are former teachers, and all
have a deep affection for this land: for its unspoiled
beauty and the release it affords from urban stresses.

We have come to know stockmen, motel owners, and saw-
mill operators. Park employees and forest rangers.
Wildlife specialists and road workers. Orchardists,
farmers, builders, artists, real estate brokers, store
owners, service station operators, politicians and
bureaucrats. We know hunters, fishers, hikers, jeepers,
boaters, photographers, painters, bikers and fliers.
Among our most interesting friends are environmentalists.

All of these people, residents and nonresidents, asso-
ciate with the land in one capacity or another. Every
one of them is a person with diverse interests, inclina-
tions, perspectives, motives. To each the land connotes
something special, be it a livelihood, a challenge to be
overcome, a source of potential profit, a desolate and
ugly landscape that repels, or a place of wonder and beauty
to be enjoyed and treasured.

In Torrey we are much more aware of being a part of
nature's universe than we ever were in the city. Nature's
manifestations envelop us. Because of abundant sub-
surface water from the canal on two sides of our lot, we
feel as though we might be overwhelmed by exuberant plants
during the growing season. Long ago we gave up trying
to keep a manicured yard (not that we ever intended to
manicure it completely).

Gloria's gardens, so conscientiously tended in the
spring, finally explode with unwanted vegetation. No
matter how often we harvest and cut, asparagus ferns pro-
liferate out of control. Cottonwood trees shower their
copious leaves, branches, twigs and fluffy cotton abun-
dantly throughout the lot. Wild grass, alfalfa, saplings

and rabbitbrush spring up everywhere, as do so-called weeds beyond count or classification.

Our lot is an aviary from March to late fall. Feisty little Brewers blackbirds come in the spring to nest in our trees and canal rushes. Their arrogant strutting, divebombing and chip-chipping amuse and annoy us. Robins nest indiscriminately on the house or in trees. Flickers attack our cedar shakes in frustration, hummingbirds explore the walls, and unwary birds of several species break their necks or stun themselves against our sunroom windows.

Always there are raucous ravens overhead, magpies and hawks - even, now and then, an eagle, a pair of turkey vultures, or a softly whooing great horned owl. Orioles, pinyon jays, larks, bluebirds and sparrows are among the other birds that visit our lot.

One year, against our better judgment, we allowed a gentle pair of barn swallows to build their mud nest under a roof overhang. Using a mirror to look into the nest, we watched their chicks hatch and grow, then sicken and die horrible deaths, eaten alive by grubs brought to them as food. This occurred before we realized what was happening.

Mule deer have given us much pleasure, after we learned (almost too late) that if we wanted our evergreens, ornamental shrubs and fruit trees to survive in unmutilated form, we must protect them with fencing. At times we have counted as many as 19 deer in our yard, browsing or reclining in the meadow grass.

Skunks have given us some very anxious hours. One year at Easter a baby skunk came into the kitchen when someone left the door open. For two near-sleepless nights we tried to entice it into a baited box-trap, finally succeeding without unfortunate incident. It was a truly beautiful creature. I took it to the town dump and set it free. Exactly one year later (on Easter!) another baby skunk burrowed its way under a wall. We repeated the identical trapping and releasing procedure with the same results after a similar period of extreme anxiety.

Darkling beatles, more appropriately known as stink bugs, are a real bother, making their presence known at awkward and embarrassing moments, and enforcing remembrance long after they have gone down the toilet or out the door. Spiders, too, believe our home is as much theirs as ours.

For several years we shared our place with Tabby, a common striped cat of great individuality and dignity. By herself Tabby could have spent many contented years with us. Unfortunately she was promiscuous, as cats are wont to be, providing us with a much larger kitten population than we or obliging neighbors could support.

One year, being desperate and not knowing how to dispose of her latest litter of two new kittens, I did something I had never done before and never will do again: I tried to asphyxiate them with exhaust from the car. The result was an agonized death for them and lasting guilt for me.

The majority of Tabby's offspring were timid and wild, never making up to us despite our sincerest efforts to be friendly. One, however, was a beautiful black and white kitten with enormous whiskers. Panda was affectionate and playful with us, so we fell in love with her, not knowing she was not a he until she proved her motherhood (so much for our ignorance of cat physiology).

No doubt we neglected Tabby, who began to sulk and withdraw. The dynasty ended not long afterwards in tragedy. Tabby abandoned a new litter to die, then — eerily and almost intentionally, it seemed to us — placed her head under the wheel of our slow-moving car. We buried her in the orchard with her babies. After giving birth to a litter of her own and raising them to self-sufficiency, Panda went off to die of some mysterious disease. Since then we have never had the heart or endurance to adopt any other animals.

Wind can be very unpleasant in Torrey. The valley is an effective wind tunnel, as attested by all the local trees, misshapen by near-constant west-to-east airflow. In winter, when mercury readings can be below zero at night (Torrey has an altitude of 6,800 feet), wind chill is far colder than that.

We found it necessary to install a long windbreak fence, designed for easy erection in fall and dismantling in spring. That fence helps greatly in keeping us warm. Only earplugs, however, preserve our sanity as the wind howls through the bare trees, and our tepee — acting as the inside of a huge drum — amplifies the noise to nerve-shattering extremes.

One winter night, when only the framework of the tepee was in place, an enormous cottonwood tree on the canal bank blew over in what seemed to us a hurricane-force wind. Roaring like an airliner at takeoff, the wind woke us up in time to hear an earthshaking crash. Fortunately only the tips of the topmost branches reached the house, but even those were sufficient to knock part of the framework askew.

The sky is an ever-intriguing spectacle. Clouds come variously from every direction, though normally from the west and very rarely from the east and north. On several occasions I have watched them approach from two or three directions simultaneously. That is an exciting if uncommon spectacle to behold. Many times at sunset the eastern sky is colored almost as dramatically as the west.

Living as we do so strategically situated in a region of such topographic and botanical diversity, we never suffer from esthetic boredom. True, the selection of paved roads is quite limited, but every mile of road affords a rich diet of scenic smorgasbord that changes as seasons and lighting change.

At one time or another, before our move to Torrey, I had traveled most of the main roads and sideroads in this West Canyonlands region – or so I thought. I believed I had seen the major scenic attractions. Little did I realize how much I had not seen, or even knew existed.

Since coming to live in Torrey in 1976, we have traveled thousands of miles in West Canyonlands and on the High Plateaus, on trips beyond memory. To be sure, many of these have been repeat trips, but always we become aware of curious or wonderful phenomena we hadn't noticed before. In a region where shapes, patterns, designs, shadings and colors, and integrated natural relationships occur in literally infinite manifestations, how could there ever be esthetic satiation or a finality to discovery?

Every chance we get, Gloria and I drive up Thousand Lake Mountain or Boulder Mountain, or through the Circle Cliffs, or to Cathedral Valley. We jolt and jounce over the rough road to the top of Miners Mountain, from which we can look down upon the gorgeous domes of Capitol Reef, and see the heavenly vision of Gloria's Ghost City (Fremont River breaks) to the north, or gaze far beyond that to Wood Bench, San Rafael Reef, and the haunting white cliffs of Hondoo country.

We have explored the top of Boulder Mountain, where Donkey Point's sublime spectacle strikes the viewer dumb. We have been to the Henry Mountains and to Burr Point, overlooking the wild gorges of the lower Dirty Devil. Hondoo country keeps beckoning us back with the majesty of

its great precipices, canyons and buttes. We have been to
Horseshoe (Barrier) Canyon, to Lands End, Panorama Point,
and down the Flint Trail to Maze Overlook. Always an
inspiration, the Waterpocket Fold and Circle Cliffs are
frequent destinations.

Quite often we drive the steep, rough road from Torrey
to the east shoulder of Thousand Lake Mountain, where the
eye encounters a mosaic of natural beauty beyond belief.
We have climbed to the top of the mountain's 11,000-foot
lava cap to gaze into the wonderland of Deep Creek Canyon
and Paradise Flats.

Many times, on Windy Ridge, we have stood in silent
awe at the center of a full circle panorama that encom-
passes, in one magnificent sweep, Cathedral Valley ...
Last Chance Desert ... San Rafael Swell ... Caineville
mesas and Factory Butte ... South Desert ... the Henry
Mountains ... northern Waterpocket Fold ... and the immense
hulk of Thousand Lake Mountain itself.

Cathedral Valley has captured us, body and soul. How
can we explain the mystic lure of that place? To us it
represents purity of earth, sky and form. Its shapes and
designs are cosmic archetypes, deeply meaningful to those
with mystical leanings. All natural designs, I suppose,
are archetypes of a sort; but those of Cathedral Valley
have an esthetic perfection all their own, and it is easy
to find striking resemblances to human art and architecture of many ages and cultures.

Such universal resemblances between natural forms and
those created by the human mind - in an area not even
known 50 years ago to more than a handful of people - are
subjects for serious ponderings. Actually, archetypal
synchronicity or parallelism of this type has been seriously considered by scholars - but never, to my knowledge,
with respect to rock designs of the Enchanted Wilderness,
where it is so very striking.

## REVELATIONS IN GEOLOGY

Geology's technical aspects still frighten me. Despite
a university geology course, the perusal of many geology
works, and months in the field, I am still an amateur.

Much of what I have learned about systematic geology
was picked up while preparing a filmstrip on the geology
of Utah; writing geology sections in several books; and
creating my film on the geology of the Colorado Plateau.
All of these were basic introductions to geology. Asso-

View eastward from Thousand Lake Mountain.

View south from Muley Point Overlook. Monument Valley in distance.

Looking west from Factory Bench.

Face of South Caineville Mesa.

ciation for three years in business with eminent teachers
of geology did little to help me in understanding the
nuances of this most complex study.

Yet I am fortunate, finally, in being able to recognize the major rock formations of the Plateau. I know
their origins, erosional characteristics, and location of
the most dramatic exposures. I can tell a monocline when
I see one, or an anticline, a swell, a dome, a fault or
joint. Igneous sills and dikes are familiar, and glacial
phenomena such as those on Boulder and Thousand Lake
mountains.

This type of recognition ability, gained primarily
during the Torrey years, adds considerably to my percep-
tual enjoyment of the Enchanted Wilderness. Rocks and
forms have become meaningful in a context of relationships. Knowledge of origins and developmental history
amplifies the fascination and intrigue of imagination,
ranging over incalculable ages. Picturing the conditions
under which rock was formed, deformed, and eroded away is
an exercise in visualizing ancient environments of great
diversity.

It is the Plateau's amazingly diversified environmental backgrounds that make it so unique today. I suppose that other places of comparable size have had geological backgrounds resembling in ways that of the Plateau, if not identical in every respect. This is indicated
by certain similarities in erosional form between the
Plateau and other parts of the world. People who are
familiar with arid terrains in Asia and Africa, or even
the badlands of Canada and the Dakotas, can point to
striking resemblances between those places and certain
geological phenomena of the Colorado Plateau.

Despite occasional similarities, however, what makes
the Plateau so overwhelmingly distinctive are uncommon
characteristics such as the following:

... The Plateau's ancient environments in which its
rocks were formed included open oceans, landlocked seas,
lakes, rivers, marshes, swamps, tidal plains, estuaries,
deserts, and ice ages. The list could be extended. At
different times the region has been below sea level, at
sea level, and at varying elevations above sea level,
rising and falling through periods of deposition, warping,
fracturing and wearing down. These periods did not occur
in every part of the Plateau at the same time or in the
same sequence.

... Being the product of greatly diversified environments, the Plateau's rocks exhibit varied personalities. They contain different minerals, different combinations of mud-silt-sand-pebbles-cobbles-etc. They are of varying degrees of hardness. Their coloration varies intricately across the spectrum.

... Because each kind of rock is so individualistic in composition, each rock or group of rocks (formations) exhibits erosional characteristics that are distinctive to that particular rock type or formation. Therefore, since literally hundreds of different rock strata (layers) were laid down on the Plateau and are exposed to weathering at this time, the result is an infinitude of rock forms and designs in an array of colors to challenge the palette of any painter.

If a person becomes familiar with only half a dozen major rock formations, he or she will add immeasurably to the viewing experience. Then, even separated areas will "pull together" with other places in relational aspects or design similarities not likely to be noted otherwise.

For example, if a person happened to be familiar with the erosional characteristics of Navajo sandstone – grand cliff faces and gently rounded domes, pinnacles, fins, mounds, slopes – similarities between the architecture of Zion National Park, the Glen Canyon-Escalante-Boulder area, the crest of Capitol Reef-Waterpocket Fold, and other places would be excitingly apparent. The Navajo is also notable for extremely narrow, notch-like canyons.

The orange-red Wingate sandstone is a foundation for the Navajo and intermediate Kayenta formation. Of all rocks in Canyonlands it is one of the most dramatic, because it forms hundreds of miles of near-vertical cliffs, including those upper-level precipices surrounding the confluence of the Green and Colorado rivers (such as at Dead Horse and Grandview points). Wingate cliffs also are prominent or dominating in Capitol Reef National Park, the lower Dirty Devil, Hondoo and Buckhorn country in the San Rafael Swell, the Circle Cliffs, Navajo country, the Moab area. Not only is the Wingate notable for the massiveness of its cliff exposures; surface sculpturing can be literally exquisite and endlessly fascinating.

Gloria and I have a special affection for the Entrada sandstone because it weathers into such an astounding variety of shapes and designs. In the west it helps to form the graceful temple-buttes and noble cliff-faces of

Cathedral Valley and South Desert. A few miles away to
the east, another segment of the Entrada exhibits in Goblin
Valley a multitude of strange forms that could hardly differ more from those of Cathedral Valley. Even farther
east, the Entrada is mother rock for the arches and fins
of Arches National Park.

The cumulative thickness of relatively youthful Cretaceous rocks is startling. These rocks are colored in
pastel shades of brown, blue, green and gray. In the
Caineville-Henry Mountains region they form enormous ter-
raced cliffs and vast areas of softly contoured badlands.

Cretaceous rocks vary greatly in hardness and thickness, so they weather into seemingly limitless forms,
shapes, and designs. For sheer magnificence it would be
hard to surpass the feathery fluting of the Caineville
mesas and Factory Butte, flaunted in immense cliff panels
hundreds of feet high and miles in length. Nearby, in
utter contrast of size and style, canyons of Factory Bench
display some of the most wonderful miniature sculpturing
to be found on the Plateau.

The Moenkopi formation also is prominent in the Plateau
region, being intermediate between the higher/younger
Navajo-Kayenta-Wingate-Chinle and the lower/older Grand
Canyon rocks (Kaibab and Coconino). This chocolate-brown
series of sedimentary rocks weathers into a fantastic
variety of three-dimensional shapes and surface reliefs.
Torrey is on the Moenkopi. Moenkopi cliffs, carved into
the most delightful fluting and buttressing, form a con-
tinuous wall between Bicknell on the west and southern
reaches of Capitol Reef, 36 miles away.

I could go on tirelessly describing the Plateau's rocks
and their personalities. There is no end to manifestations of inorganic art in this region. If we could devote
the remainder of our days to doing nothing but examining
this art, we would never exhaust nature's repertory of
strange, beautiful, exotic, grotesque-bizarre, exquisite,
delightful, you-name-it shapes and designs.

All the illustrations ever published on this region -
collectively, in total - give but the slightest suggestion
of what art is here for the seeking out and experiencing.

*Part Five*

# THE VISION:
# A MILLENNIAL DREAM

I am talking to you: my fellow, anyone. This is
your country, your land! Embrace it. Protect it.
Know it. I want you to know!

Do you seek peace, beauty, soul? Come, enter in,
you who care. We have an affinity. Now, today.
I speak to you!

*Gloria*

In 1975, the year before our Torrey move, Gloria and I
spent some weeks in Europe with my sister-in-law Beverly.
We visited Italy, Switzerland and France, making our own
way. That year was Roman Catholic Holy Year, an occasion
that brought pilgrims to Rome from all over the world.

We, too, were pilgrims of a sort, marveling at the
architectural, symbolic products of faith, devotion and
renaissance enlightenment that make a European tour so
rewarding. Being beauty-sensitive to an uncommon degree,
and empathetic with devotees of whatever religious per-
suasion, Gloria especially was overwhelmed.

We visited sanctuaries in Rome, Florence and Venice;
drove to Switzerland, where we spent a week; and then
stayed a few days in Paris and Chartres. Cathedral architecture has always fascinated me and Gloria, especially
the Gothic, because it represents humanity's inspired
attempts to combine the mortal and divine in material form.

Chartres was a special goal for us. We arrived on a
bitter-cold day without adequate clothing, hungry and almost
penniless, with no money to buy food after purchasing our
train tickets. None of us will forget that day, for several reasons, not least of which was the mystic impact of
the cathedral itself. Beverly kept thinking of a new wallet her daughter had given her as a going away present.
When we arrived back at our room in Paris, she opened the

wallet and found $15 that Trudy had tucked inside. That night we ate. Next day we flew back to Utah.

In 1982 we joined a LaMar Berrett tour to the Holy Land and Egypt. LaMar is the epitome of a tour guide: brimming over with vitality, efficiency, information, and love for his subject. Also he believes in wasting not a minute. All of us, therefore, returned exhausted if fulfilled. In three weeks he took us to London, Vienna, Israel, Egypt and Greece, after which Gloria and I returned to London for an additional week's stay.

Two years later we spent more than a month in Nepal and India. Expecting to join a group in India, we arrived in Delhi to find we were on our own, though arrangements had been made for us. Suffice to say that we saw the Himalayas, climbing a low ridge to view the indescribable Annapurna massif in full face and at close range. We visited many of the historic and sacred places of northern India, from Varanasi (Benares) on the Ganges to Mount Abu and Ranakpur in Rajasthan.

## A STATE AND AN IMAGE

I mention those trips because they influenced profoundly my attitude, and Gloria's, toward Utah and the Enchanted Wilderness. Travel broadens. It also transforms and enlightens. Ways of seeing things change, if imperceptibly at times.

The European visit of 1975 was not my first, but I did perceive Europe with eyes that were 20 years older and wiser. During those 20 years I had concentrated my attention somewhat exclusively on Utah and the western states.

The Utah culture is very young by Old World standards, still not fully assimilated (mediocratized) by the voracious, all-consuming American culture. A few distinctive cultural traits remain, though these may be difficult to detect or define in cases.

When I began my Utah work in the 1940s, the state's culture was much more distinctive and original than it is today. Nearly a hundred years of geographic isolation had allowed its peculiar brew of diverse nationality/societal origins and customs to simmer without the interfering influences that many other states endured.

I have watched and participated in the transformation from a provincial, staid, isolated, self-conscious community of a half-million souls to a confident, dynamic, growing, outward-looking segment of a national, even an international society. The population has tripled, and most of these added people are clustered tightly along the Wasatch Front.

Urbanization is the order of the day in Utah today, as it is in most other places around the world. So, too, is "modernization" in architecture, lifestyles, transportation, industry, and other aspects of existence.

Nowdays the "past" is hardly visible to the eye. Very few people who were born in the last century are even alive today, and relatively few buildings from that era still exist. Those that do are curiosities of a sort.

As for the land itself, compared with the majority of states, Utah remains relatively a near-wild region, if "wild" is used in a comparative, non-technical sense. About three-fourths of this land, held by federal or state governments or Indian tribes, remains in an undeveloped or little developed stage. Most of it is likely never to see much development because of lack of water, useful minerals, forage, timber, or because of climate and other factors.

I emphasize likely. As discussed in Part Six, the most unlikely things may occur or be proposed in future: witness the MX missile basing proposal, Kaiparowits and Intermountain power projects, oil shale and tar sands, nuclear waste repository, Great Salt Lake pumping into the west desert - even Lake Powell and Flaming Gorge Reservoir. No area is really immune from change.

However that may be, urban Utah of today bears slight physical resemblance to the Utah of 30 or 40 years ago. Even the great Wasatch peaks are obscured many days, five months of the year, by fog and smog. And the most irritating concomitants of population density - traffic congestion, pollution, crowding, crime and other social problems - tend to counterbalance the advantages of urban living. Nevertheless, Utah is still fortunate in possessing what could fairly be termed a good quality of life for the majority of its people.

A wealth of open space still surrounds the metropolitan areas, relieving urban pressures to an extent for people who are able and willing to get in a car and drive into the countryside.

... What came to me in 1975 in Zurich, Switzerland, with powerful impact, was the conviction that **Utah is rapidly going the way of every other urbanized society.** And it is doing so willingly, eagerly, purposefully - and ignorantly!

Here I was in Zurich's railroad station, jostled and engulfed by crowds of people dashing frantically in all directions. The scene was pure bedlam. I couldn't walk two steps without being blocked or forced to dodge somebody. The noise was unendurable.

Was that the situation toward which Utahns were moving so inexorably? Could it really be? Assuredly it was.

I was overcome with a sense of mission. I would devote my life to a crusade against such blindness. Utah was different! Utah had intelligent, educated people. Utah was blessed with visionary, idealistic citizens and leaders. Utah had a cultural and natural birthright of a high order.

Utah need not follow well worn paths threading the mazes of ignorance and undirection that had entrapped other societies through the ages. It could set new directions for western America if not the world. It was superior!

Alas. Sense of mission is often tenuous and not always capable of overcoming circumstance.

I was forced to admit that the Utah of my ideals did not correspond with reality. In actuality, the majority of Utahns and their leaders seem to accept the "Growth for Growth's Sake" philosophy, with hardly a question as to the ultimate results or desirability of such a philosophy. So far as I know, decision makers and movers in Utah have no alternative philosophy at all, or none that has been promulgated widely.

Utah's leaders cheer enthusiastically when census figures show one of the highest growth rates of any state, and the highest birth rate, at the same time that leaders in many countries are doing everything possible to lower birth rates.

Cries of joy are heard when some new building or industrial project is announced. Local, state and regional economic development agencies spend huge sums in the attempt to lure new industry and more people to Utah. Every exploitable or potentially exploitable resource is eyed, probed, put to immediate use wherever possible. (In the past this was done without regard to accompanying consequences; such haphazardness is not quite the case today, thank heaven.)

Now, I do not claim omniscience or omnipotence. I have

no all-wise answers or solutions. And I make no blanket condemnation of urbanization per se, which seems to be an irresistible wave of present and future. What I say here is that I witnessed in Zurich – and in London, Paris, Rome, New York, Delhi, Bombay, Cairo, Athens and every other big city on our itineraries – the frightful consequences of extreme, out-of-control urbanization.

Do Utah's leaders and its people actually envy and wish to emulate these other places? Do they try to learn from the mistakes of others and attempt to avoid the pitfalls encountered by other urban communities that have moved ahead more rapidly, and perhaps more carelessly? After all, Utah has not customarily been in the forefront as an innovator of societal change. It tends to be a follower, an imitator, or even a laggard compared with more dynamic cultures such as those on the west coast or the Sun Belt.

Followers, one would think, would not make the same missteps as leaders.

I have come to the conclusion that learning from the mistakes of other societies is not a common trait among Utah's leaders, movers and doers. Otherwise they would hesitate in their pell-mell rush to apply the same programs, or lack of programs, that are culminating in social disasters now so apparent around the world. They would take stock, scrutinize their programs, goals and objectives; analyze potential consequences; decide whether programs, goals and objectives ought not to be modified.

Above all, it seems to me, leaders should tune in their collective vision and try to see what they would like Utah to be 20, 30 or 50 years down the road. Without such collective vision as a goal, nothing closely resembling it is likely to be achieved.

During much of my Utah career I have taken pride in our state's governmental, educational, economic, social and religious communities. I have felt confident that Utah's leaders generally were forward-looking, intelligent, idealistic, honest, even visionary to a marked extent. I suppose that many of them really do rank fairly high on that demanding scale, for urban communities in Utah are not the most backward in the country – and, in fact, they exhibit many admirable qualities.

Whether these positive qualities are as admirable and as encompassing as they ought to be is the question. I do not believe they are, and the reasons – in my opinion – are due to a lack of collective vision in the entire society, but principally on levels of leadership.

I must say in sadness: Utahns collectively, as a non-sectarian culture, have no **Proud Image** of their place in the world. And they have no **Grand Dream.**

Serious questions about Images and Dreams took definite form in my mind in 1976, a few months before we moved to Torrey. (Gloria has always contributed her insights to mine.) The proposed Kaiparowits power project in southern Utah had been studied in an exhaustive environmental impact statement which described a host of sobering environmental effects on a remote, uninhabited wilderness, as well as the certainty of air degradation in the Glen Canyon basin – if not the entire basin of the Colorado River in the Canyonlands region – not to mention the necessity of erecting transmission lines across hundreds of miles of wide-open country to southern California and southern Arizona.

Though eventually abandoned because of excessive cost and other factors, before that decision was announced the project was enthusiastically supported by Utah's congressional delegation, state administration, and – according to a poll by Senator Moss – the majority of people in Utah. Why? Because it would provide an economic boost to southern Utah (notably Kane County), would increase state tax revenue, and would represent "progress". No matter that generated power was destined primarily for bloated, energy-voracious metropolitan areas in other states, or that another giant step in the industrialization of a wilderness **unique in the world** would be taken.

That reasoning angered me and Gloria. With her help I wrote a five-page open letter entitled "HERITAGE FOR SALE ... Any bid accepted ... Money is the only object" and mailed it to several hundred state legislators, public officials, political candidates, and prominent citizens.

As I recall, two or three of those people acknowledged that open letter. (Such a response would be considered poor in a commercial mail-order solicitation.) I assume most copies were not even read, or if they were, were shrugged off as the musings of a crank. Small wonder: We accused Utah of being a benighted state in serious respects.

That was no "sour grapes" opinion. We based it on the following points:

1. Utahns (speaking of the large majority) had little conception of the uniqueness of their state's natural and cultural heritage. Or so it appeared to us. Lacking in

Desert varnish in Long Canyon, Circle Cliffs (along the so-called Burr Trail).

such concept, they had little realization or appreciation
of the value of such a distinctive heritage in today's
world. Instead of treasuring this endowment as worthy of
the most deliberate husbanding, they were willing and
anxious to sell it for a mess of economic pottage. The
state's relative salvation to date was the result less of
ideals than of the scarcity or inattention of those who
could exploit its resources.

2. Degradation of clean air ... mutilation of the
countryside and canyons ... development of some of the
most outstanding scenic areas in America with incompatible industries ... construction of paved highways through
wild areas when the need had not been justified ...
demolition of a good part of the state's architectural
heritage and replacement by commonplace structures. Those
happenings were accepted more or less passively by the
majority of Utahns, who regarded them as necessary steps
along the road of Progress.

3. Utahns in general had the attitude that the natural
resources within the state's borders belonged to them, or
at least that Utahns should have some sort of priority
"say" concerning their disposition, or a priority right to
their exploitation. That was nonsense and arrogance. For
130 years, white Utahns had survived economically on land
that belongs, largely, to the nation as a whole.

It appeared to us, furthermore, that the majority of
Utahns had a greater conviction than ever that their
rights to and opinions about the public domain had some
sort of God-given sanctity, far transcending rights of the
other 99½ percent of Americans who own two-thirds of
Utah's land.

4. There appeared to be no shame or remorse for past
abuses of the environment. On the contrary, most Utahns
seemed perfectly willing, anxious and determined to inflict
the same degradation on a part of Utah which did not even
belong to them, which few of them had ever seen, and about
which they cared little except for the dollars that would
accrue.

5. Finally, though the natural wonders of the state
had long been a piece of the economic cake for a good part
of the population, Senator Moss's survey showed that most
Utahns were perfectly willing - even anxious and determined
- to "trade off" some of the glory of those natural wonders
for a relatively few industrial jobs and tax dollars. This
was to be done primarily (or ostensibly) for the economic
benefit of five percent of the state's population and 1/40th

of one percent of the nation's. (More than 80 percent of
the land in southern Utah is federally owned.)

We were not being facetious with that title "Heritage
for sale". With relatively few exceptions, Utahns and
their leaders had always been willing – even eager –
to trade their heritage for economic pottage. What had
happened to their scale of values? Or had they ever
established a scale of values for the state's environmental
and cultural heritage?

However unusual the heritage, whether natural, cultural
or historical, the guiding philosophy was: put it to immediate economic use, whether or not such use destroyed or
mutilated that heritage. Future generations be damned.
Let them fend for themselves. That moving philosophy of
powers-that-be applied in Utah as in the nation until
very recent years, when a degree of restraint has become
discernible.

Whether Utahns are any greedier or shortsighted in
this respect than citizens of other states is beside the
point.

What is needed to modify those undesirable traits of
collective Utah society? I can only offer suggestions,
but I believe those are essential to significant change
in directions:

**Utah needs Inspiring Leadership!** Officials must **lead,
inspire, enlighten,** show a better way of doing things.
Religious leaders attempt to do those things with respect
to ethical and moral attitudes and behavior. Political,
educational, social and economic leaders should do likewise with respect to secular attitudes and behavior.

**Utah needs Unprecedented Vision and Action.** Advancement
comes by hesitant half-steps, hardly ever by leaps and
bounds. Yet the attainment of worthwhile goals requires
pre-vision. Seldom are they reached by blind accident.

The entire world is entering a new age. Can that be
doubted? Old ways of doing things are no longer adequate.
There are tremendous new challenges. Who would question
that?

The call today is for vision and action on unprecedented
levels of practical and theoretical intelligence. The
very concept of Progress is undergoing radical redefinition.
Values are changing. The "good life" has different meanings today than it had yesterday.

People are asking: Just what **is** worthwhile development?
How do you **control** growth, and to what extent? Probably
the majority of people are not yet asking those questions,
but a goodly number are.

Visions of attainable grandeur are hardly to be expected
from the general public in the form of suggested Goals, or
in platforms of political parties, or the acts (however
sincere) of elected officials and legislators. What is
needed above all are the ideas of **Thinkers** and professional
**Doers**: those who have faced far more serious problems than
Utah and have a practical basis from which to suggest
appropriate solutions or remedies.

**Utah needs a Proud Image.** Ask yourself: Just what **is**
Utah's image in the world? In the national mind? In the
minds of its own people?

Imperial Rome had a world image. The British Empire
had a world image. The United States of America has
changing and diversified world images.

Oregon ... California ... New York ... Texas ... New
Mexico ... Arizona ... even Nevada. These states have
strong images in the collective national mind, if not the
international mind. Can Utah say the same? After the
expenditure of multiple millions of advertising dollars,
what is Utah's image?

What would Utahns like their state's image to be?
Great Salt Lake? Is that an attractive image? (For that
matter, does the name Salt Lake City create an attractive
image?) Mormon Temple Square? Is that an accurate or
appropriate image for the state? Home of the Mormons?
What do non-Mormons in Utah think of that?

When Utah's people have only a hazy image of their
state, and uncertain aspirations, how can those serve as a
beacon?

I suggest, as a contribution to the search for a proud
and meaningful image, that Utahns take serious stock of
what place or thing within the state's boundaries is
truly incomparable in the world. Something of which all
Utahns could and should be immensely proud. Something
they would treasure with genuine passion if only they got
to know it better; then they would keep that treasure
inviolate from incompatible or inappropriate uses.

**Only one place in the state meets those specifications.**
That place is Utah's part of the Colorado Plateau.

The Swiss have their Alps, and they have made of those wonderful mountains - even where development has occurred - a nationwide park.

England reveres and protects its historical heritage and its gorgeous green landscape. Holland flaunts its tulips and its windmills. Paris is a shrine not only to Parisians but to the world. The monuments of Rome have been a beacon for more than 2,000 years. Skyscrapers are the pride of New York City, Hong Kong and Sao Paulo. San Francisco has its bay, its bridges and hills. Many cities of Europe are tenderly preserved as living museums.

Nepal has the grandest mountains on earth. Some are holy to its people, the abode of their gods.

What have Utahns created or preserved that can be flaunted proudly before the world? There are positive answers here, but let the reader reflect upon them.

**Even beyond those, <u>What does Utah possess that stands alone, by itself, matchless, superb and superlative, without equal or counterpart</u>?**

*That place, of course, is Utah's part of the Colorado Plateau. Canyonlands and the High Plateaus. The Enchanted Wilderness. It is blindness and folly to ignore the potential and suitability of that region as an inspirational symbol for the state.*

## A MILLENNIAL DREAM

It goes without saying that Utahns are not the only ones
who give little environmental consideration to proposals
for economic development in the Colorado Plateau. Citizens of the Plateau's other three states are just as anxious
for development, if not moreso. Their eagerness is as understandable as that of residents in Utah's part of the
Plateau.

Thousands of people live on the Plateau in Arizona, New
Mexico, and Colorado. They must survive somehow. At the
same time, the Plateau in those other states (with exceptions) is not as scenically unusual as it is in parts of
southern Utah, where Canyonlands and the High Plateaus comprise most of the Plateau within Utah.

The New World and Millennial Dream concepts were described in Issue No. 1 of the *Enchanted Wilderness Magazine*.
They were emotional and visionary, impractical in respects
but not completely unattainable in reality.

At the time I wrote that editorial and article at the
end of 1970, Gloria and I were on a "high" of animation
and enthusiasm. Only one year into the Natural History
Inc. enterprise, we were crossing the threshold of the
Enchanted Wilderness stage. We were still optimistic and
excited. While as enthusiastic now as then, we are
16 years older and lack the physical vitality of those
days. Younger, more vigorous crusaders are carrying the
fight. We can only help to pass the ammunition.

I cannot improve on the New World vision of those days,
so I reproduce it here unchanged:

## A NEW WORLD

This maiden issue of *The Enchanted Wilderness Magazine* is designed as an introduction to a New World.

Not a New World in obvious ways, of course, for this
is a very old, very ancient world that reveals the
pages of geological time in an almost unbroken sequence
for more than a billion years. The "feel" of relative
eternity is a pervading, even oppressive atmosphere
in the Enchanted Wilderness. Evidences of life all
the way up from its primeval beginnings have been found
here. And numerous cultures have left their marks
throughout this land, some in rich abundance.

Still, as an original concept of "Enchanted Wilderness" this is a new world. Until now the Colorado
Plateau as a unit...as an integral whole...as a dis-
tinct physiographic province...has not been recognized
by more than a handful of visionary people as a world
resource, a unique wilderness of true enchantment.
Heretofore, "wilderness" to most people has meant the
remote fastnesses of lofty mountain ranges, or unvio-
lated pockets of wild lands scattered here and there.
But how many have been aware that the Colorado Plateau
is the largest wild or near-wild province still remaining in the 48 contiguous states - a vast and, until
recently, little known region larger than the State of
New Mexico and containing fewer than a half million
inhabitants?

Who has had the vision to evaluate this natural
World Shrine at its actual and potential worth - not
as a shattered entity broken up into political subdiv-
isions, exploited haphazardly and ruthlessly for its
removable and manipulative resources, but rather as an
integral, homogeneous *wilderness* having similar but
extraordinary physical characteristics over much of its
great extent?

Who has had the vision (even a faint glimmer) to recognize the incalculable future worth of the Colorado Plateau as a *region* - not as bits and pieces of isolated parks...not as a golden opportunity for indiscriminate industrial exploitation and expanding urbanization...not as a newly-discovered playground for uncontrolled travel and recreation...but as a precious *wilderness*, valuable to the world for its peace and loneliness as well as its minerals, for its inspiring beauty and strange enchantment as well as its boundless opportunities for physical recreation?

A few people have had this exciting vision. It is our dream to increase their numbers. EWA's stated goal is "the preservation of the unique attributes of the Colorado Plateau and its Borderlands - the Enchanted Wilderness - through enlightened public awareness and controlled utilization of its priceless resources."

In the Millennial Dream article I described the Enchanted Wilderness - the Colorado Plateau and its borderlands - "as it is and ought to be".

EWA's founders, I said, recognized the uniqueness of that region and loved it with a nostalgic love similar in kind and intensity to the love of the Swiss for their Alps, or the English for the green rusticity of their native land.

These founders recognized that if they wished to influence how the world looked at the Colorado Plateau (a name that is not very descriptive or emotionally captivating to the unknowing public), they must communicate in words which the world would understand and respond to emotionally. "Fortunately, the Colorado Plateau could be described in such words: it was 'enchanted' as much as any region could be enchanted, and it certainly was a 'wilderness' for the most part."

Names have a magic about them. "If people identify a name with an object, the name and the object in effect become the same thing; people view them as identical and will resist change. In the case of the Enchanted Wilderness, hopefully the world will learn to consider this region emotionally as an enchanted land and will resist anything that detracts from this image. Likewise, if they are aware that it is still a wilderness (an emotional concept that becomes continually less forbidding and more inviting to more people), those who place a positive value on wilderness will resist anything that threatens to change this image."

My article continued as follows:

"In today's frantic world of oppressive urbanization, natural enchantment and unspoiled wilderness are becoming rare and precious commodities. And they promise to become more rare and precious still, long before the rape of America's landscape has been halted.

"Perhaps it is a miracle that the Colorado Plateau and its borderlands have remained so relatively unspoiled for so long. How could such a vast region remain such a little-populated backwater in the rushing westward tide of empire? When metropolitan concentrations on three sides of the Colorado Plateau are among the fastest-growing urban areas in the nation, what has kept the Plateau's population and its economic development at such a static level? . . .

"The reasons are easy to identify, but three of them rank far ahead of others as the main causes of low population and slow development. These are the lack of utilizable water, the extreme ruggedness of the terrain, and the lack of suitable agricultural land.

"What is of greater interest here is the very fact that such an immense region of such remarkable natural attributes still remains in such a comparatively wild condition in the midst of such a rapidly-growing concentration of millions of affluent and mobile people!

"Such an anomaly deserves very serious consideration from every quarter - much more than it has yet received.

"It deserves much more coordination of planning and action among the numerous government and Indian agencies that control from 56% to 87% of the Colorado Plateau, depending on state.

"The region's wilderness and recreational attributes deserve vastly more concern from planners and developers at all levels of government and private enterprise. Local residents in particular, with few exceptions, are pitifully unaware of the potential of these attributes, and also woefully derelict in taking positive action to profit economically from them.

"Planners and developers seem to concentrate on every industrial potential except the wilderness and recreational possibilities, which certainly exceed other industries by far in ultimate potential. . . .

"This is not to imply there is no official concern for preservation of environment or the ultimate quality of life in the region. Of course there is. . . .

"Nevertheless, there is a scarcity of far-horizon vision
in positions of influence. Too little attention is paid
to non-economic values as these seem to be emerging among
enlightened segments of America's population. Promotion
is too non-selective. Too much stress is given to increasing volume instead of quality.

"Is our Enchanted Wilderness to be destroyed bit by
bit, attribute by attribute, through this inadequately
planned, little-coordinated, ultimately senseless expoita-
tion of a priceless world resource?

"Today's world cries ever more loudly for natural sanctuaries, for spiritual and emotional uplift that can only
be experienced far away from urban tensions. Tomorrow's
'global village' - more particularly our 'American village'
- will find indispensable its few remaining natural clois-
ters, places of delight and wonder for rehabilitation of
the harried soul.

"The Enchanted Wilderness of the Colorado Plateau still
remains a natural sanctuary of the highest order. No one
with knowledge of the region can deny this.

"This last finally brings us to definitions, those
irritating little things that cause so much dissension.
Just what comprises 'violation' of this precious land?
What are its valid uses?

"The purpose of this article is not to propose workable
definitions, which can only be established through sincere discussion, mutual goodwill, compromise, and court
decisions, all requiring many years. . . .

"As a beginning, EWA starts with a fairly non-contro-
versial premise: that controlled travel and recreation are
the highest uses to which much of the Enchanted Wilderness
should be devoted in the future - not always to the exclusion of other uses, but certainly to the degree of making
these 'highest uses' the common denominator for measuring
desirability of other uses."

Issue No. 1 of the magazine was the first and last.
Printed magazines became too expensive for us, so we substituted modest bulletins for reporting developments or planned developments in the Plateau and its borderlands. We
quoted piquant, relevant comments from other sources. We
amplified on the Enchanted Wilderness concept.

As our strength ebbed, we did what we could to encourage regional planning and zoning. I described the idea to

Senator Frank Moss, who was more responsible politically than anybody else during the 1960s and early 1970s for establishing and enlarging national parks and monuments in Canyonlands, as well as Glen Canyon National Recreation Area. I cannot say how genuine his interest was, but he did promise to consider introducing legislation if EWA would submit a draft for staff study.

We never did. EWA breathed its last, and our lives – of necessity – went in other directions. Before that happened I expanded in writing on the Millennial Dream, in an item mailed to members. Nobody commented, so I do not know whether a common chord was struck. Perhaps by then I was in the clouds, far from reality. Readers can judge for themselves:

### A MILLENNIAL DREAM (continued)

"The vision grows. The dream of a New World continues, interrupted by painful interludes of reality, but unlike most dreams not evaporating completely as the demands of mortality lay daily claim to one's conscious facilities.

"Who has dreamed of a New World in the Colorado Plateau? . . .

"Here in the Enchanted Wilderness of the Colorado Plateau is dream material to animate an entire nation if only there were dreamers enough to catalyze the whole!

"Here is an almost virgin land...a truly unique land... in some respects a land choice above all other lands.

"This little-spoiled land is just over the threshold of certain exploitation. Will it go the way of other lands that man has 'developed' all around it? Is it to succumb to his avarice and shortsightedness?

"Not completely, we can be fairly sure – but only because so much of it is still retained by federal and state governments. . . .

"The wilderness preservation movement has fought many a battle during the past 60 or 70 years, winning quite a few, losing others. Battles are still being fought, of course, and the preservation struggle will never cease. *A major engagement in this struggle could be the fight for the Colorado Plateau.* I say 'could be' because there is so little general realization now of what is ultimately involved.

"Am I being melodramatic? Perhaps, but I think not.

"Bringing this dream of an everlasting Enchanted Wilderness into being is much too forbidding a project for me or my immediate coworkers – but it is not impossible of accomplishment for hundreds and thousands of dreamers, all working together in a great missionary effort to influence the people who make those critical decisions that could soon mutilate this magnificently unique heritage of all mankind.

". . . There is not even a moderate degree of coordination between the diverse federal-state-county-Indian-commercial-agricultural-and other interests involved in planning and development of the Colorado Plateau.

"In other words, here is a little-developed void in the heart of the rapidly growing West – a unique world in itself – a challenge to the highest planning and visionary aspirations of enlightened modern society. Society has the vision and the ability to do with this region whatever it collectively wants to do with it!

"Here is an epochal opportunity for society to put into effect a significant part of what utopian dreamers have dreamed about for centuries. Here is a New World waiting to be planned and molded. Will society exploit it ruthlessly and haphazardly as it has done with every other man-handled world in the past?

"I do not make the slightest suggestion that the Enchanted Wilderness should be 'locked up' in the strict sense. Trying to do this would be only a useless delaying tactic. (This is not to negate the efforts of dedicated souls who fight power plant pollution, the despoliation of certain natural sanctuaries that ought to be preserved inviolate, the construction of hard-topped highways into every nook and corner of the region, the damming of every free stream. Their work has been and will be vital to realization of the grand plan.)

"*What I am suggesting here is that a major campaign could be waged to save the entire region through formal planning and zoning – not alone for the present generation, most of whom do not know and appreciate it, but for our descendants, who will know and treasure it.*

"I am suggesting that a few dozen national parks and monuments, a few score state parks, several recreation areas, several designated wild areas, a handful of BLM campgrounds, and our precious national forests will not suffice in this region for the future.

"I am suggesting that uncontrolled, unimaginative,

unesthetic private developments now underway around the
Plateau region are indicative of gross negligence on the
part of their builders and the officials who could and
should regulate them. . . .

"Ideally, what the Colorado Plateau needs is a master
planner, a visionary genius having an unparalleled background of education, training and experience in multiple
disciplines. . . . If, in addition to superhuman vision,
idealism, wisdom and knowledge, this master planner also
possessed unlimited police and political power, as well
as boundless financial resources, he could do a fair job
of creating a utopia in the Plateau.

"If no single person possesses all of these qualities
and powers - or even more than a few of them - that is not
to say that a significant number could not be made available and utilizable through some type of collective arrange-
ment such as a high-level regional Planning Council.

"Councils already exist by the hundreds, for a great
variety of purposes, bringing together multiple talents
and powers for resolving complex situations. . . .

"[Such a council] could be made to work, even if only
clumsily at first - and any success at all in coordinating
and controlling the multiplicity of plans and activities
in this region would justify its existence.

"Without becoming too unwieldy, a regional Planning
Council could be devised to fairly represent government
and other interests. Above all the Council should be
non-political in makeup and should operate free from the
vagaries of national, state and local politics.

"*The greatest minds should be invited to think upon
what the Enchanted Wilderness should and could mean to
mankind, and give their opinions freely as a gift, without
fee. Such an invitation would be regarded as a privilege
by most great thinkers. . . .*"

There was more, but that is the gist of our final mes-
sage to members on the subject of the Millennial Dream.
If the regional planning proposal was unrealistic under
the circumstances, theoretically it was not an impossi-
bility. Perhaps (I will not say probably) it was not
meant to be. Perhaps it is meant to be.

Now and then we detect faint glimmers of a happening, a
movement, a suggestion hinting at cooperative and intelligent resolution of controversies bearing on the developmental fate of the Plateau.

Designs on the wall of Long Canyon, Circle Cliffs
(along the so-called Burr Trail).

*Part Six*

# DIRECTION AND INDIRECTION

*Greed and stupidity are destroying the canyonlands.*
*Every new road, every new power plant, every new*
*real estate development means a definite and prob-*
*ably permanent loss to what should be a national or*
*even international treasure.*

Edward Abbey

## DESECRATION

In 1970 and 1971 the view from Dead Horse Point was
unalterably mutilated by the construction of a series of
immense solar evaporation ponds several miles to the east
of the point.

I wrote an article in EWA's Bulletin No. 2 (August
1971) entitled "The Incredible Desecration of Dead Horse
Point". For me the ponds had removed something precious
from my life. They were an emotional blow of traumatic
force. Never since have I been able to glance more than
momentarily in their direction the very few times I have
returned to the point.

What stirred my indignation even more than the ponds
was the blatant coverup by government officials of what
was being planned on public lands – an industrial intrusion
of major magnitude on the views from Dead Horse Point,
Island in the Sky, Hurrah Pass and Anticline Overlook. It
was a fact that federal, state and private officials – in
a complex maneuver – had transferred public land to private
use, without advertised public hearings and in the absence
of media coverage that might have let the interested public
or conservation groups know of the impending impact on
state and national parks.

The Moab newspaper responded with fury and a scathing

personal attack in response to my implication of a local media coverup, listing a series of articles about plans for the project which had appeared in that paper. Curiously, I found, not one of the quoted articles I was able to locate had mentioned specifically the ponds' proximity to or visibility from the parks. Reports in Salt Lake City newspapers likewise neglected to disclose that information. Also, I was told on good authority, officials involved were gleeful about having slipped the project past environmentalists who would have objected had they known what was in the offing.

Suffice to say that our complaints received a good deal of newspaper and television coverage. Governor Rampton wrote us a long letter, justifying the land transfer but also admitting that better ways should be found "to review the respective values, to get the public attitudes, and to better permit those with whom the power of decision is vested to make reasonable judgments."

The governor said he had issued an Executive Order requiring two public hearings when any state construction is proposed; the Department of Natural Resources had established an Ecological Review Board; the State Planning Coordinator had proposed a procedure for clearing all environmental studies in all divisions of state government through a common clearing house. He asked for suggestions on a crucial question: How can state agencies receive input from the public?

Would that federal land managers had been so responsive!

Primary justifications, of course (from the mining company, federal and state officials, and media), were that the potash operation would have had to shut down if the ponds had not been built, throwing many local people out of work; also that the esthetic effect of the ponds was debatable.

Both arguments, it seems to me, were cynical. The ponds could have been built several miles to the north, out of sight of the parks, while esthetics could have been debated before the fact if public hearings had been held before the ponds were built.

The Dead Horse Point episode is a fitting introduction to a chapter on Direction and Indirection. It illustrates graphically how the Enchanted Wilderness has been and likely will continue to be nibbled away by self-serving interests of varying nature and differing motives, using any tactic that promises success.

## OMENS

Back in 1970 and 1971 the Colorado Plateau was under heavy developmental attack. Plans were underway to make it the site of a number of behemoth coal-fired power plants. Uranium mining was approaching another zenith. Hundreds of miles of scenic parkways were planned to "open up" the entire Colorado River wilderness between Moab and the Arizona line. Myriad agencies and private entrepreneurs were making their individual plans for the area, with no coordination and no regional vision of **what ought to be** – the age-old scenario for developing a new frontier.

Has the situation changed since then? Yes, it has, for the worse in some respects but not entirely so. And there have been definite gains.

Fate decreed a developmental hiatus of sorts. Only a few of the grandiose power plants were actually built. Planned parkways never came into being. The uranium industry foundered. Formal wilderness areas have been established on national forests, and BLM wilderness areas are being studied and debated.

Threats do continue, however – insidious threats backed by powerful economic and political interests. These interests scheme behind the scenes, manipulating decisions in their favor, avoiding public confrontation wherever possible, knowing where power lies and how to exert it. These interests are ruthless. Insisting that they work for the good of the public at large, in effect they may only represent narrow special interests.

This may be a harsh generalization. It should be assumed in fairness that most political leaders _believe_ they represent the ultimate best interests of the majority of people in Utah, if not the nation, when they plan the fate of a matchless region that belongs to all humankind, not only of this generation but those who are to come afterwards. Yet, it seems to me, idealism based on concern for the land or for the benefit of more enlightened future generations is sorely lacking.

Personally I detect little long-range or lofty vision among those who make decisions regarding this land. I see few signs that they truly realize the uniqueness, fragility, or esthetic and spiritual values of the Enchanted Wilderness. Let me document a few reasons for my negativity.

1. At this writing, the Department of Energy is

seriously considering a site at the entrance to The Needles district of Canyonlands National Park as a suitable location for extensive characterization study (drilling, etc.) to determine geological suitability as a repository for nuclear waste.

Whether or not such tests ever are conducted, that grotesque proposal - on its very face - is a severe blow to the very foundational principles on which the national park system was established.

That a government of all the people would even consider such a location for such a purpose is incomprehensible.

Utah's congressional delegation did not express immediate outrage, or even a degree of moral opposition on principle. Such fence-sitting passivity or latent opportunism was not really surprising, because it had been apparent for some time that those senators and representatives lacked profound sensitivity to the esthetic, spiritual and symbolic values of the red-rock country.

2. Utah's entire congressional delegation, together with a majority of state legislators, the governor, and officials in southern Utah recently supported the proposed expenditure of more than $20 million (perhaps, ultimately, double that amount) to construct a new 66-mile paved road through near-wild terrain in southern Utah.

Supposedly responsible public officials and legislators willingly supported a construction project of that magnitude without public hearings, prior to completion of an environmental study by the National Park Service, and in the absence of serious analysis of economic costs-versus-benefits, true need, possible alternatives, and effects on other communities in the area. They also disregarded the gross pork-barrel nature of the project at a time of extreme federal budgetary stress.

Enough public and political pressure was brought to delay hard-surfacing of the entire route for a time, though the project's final status is in doubt. Whatever that may be, of greatest concern to me and Gloria is what has been evidenced by this affair: Powerful political forces in Utah and Washington are perfectly willing to "do their own thing" without soliciting widespread public opinion, making certain the project is in the general public interest (as opposed to local and business interests), or even allowing time or opportunity for opponents to inform legislators, officials, and the public at large of the many issues involved.

The Burr Trail switchbacks down a cliff from the tree
in foreground to valley below.  Peaks of the Henry
Mountains in distance (top photo).  Lower photo:  Calf
Creek Canyon in the upper Escalante region.

To us, this case indicates political contrivance, callowness and hypocrisy.

3. During congressional hearings on forest wilderness legislation in 1984, it was evident that the state's congressional delegation had little profound empathy for wilderness values, or even for the concept of wilderness. Without the assistance of non-Utahns in Congress, wilderness supporters in Utah would have lost much more than they did. The merits of acreages included or not included may be debated until kingdom-come. What I emphasize here is the ungenerous attitude of the state's delegation toward wilderness _per se_: they were dragged protesting, as it were, along the way.

Granting that senators and congressmen were politicians, sensitive to diverse interests, official bias against "locking up" much land in wilderness was evident in this case as it always has been in Utah. Multiple use has always been preferable to official and rural Utah, no matter if overriding values clearly are esthetic or recreational.

In nearly all cases, when creation or expansion of national parks or recreation areas have been proposed, public officials in Utah - with some exceptions - have come down on the side of multiple use and "less is best". The same can be said for development agencies such as chambers of commerce.

4. One other example illustrates how the Plateau is being nibbled away, and how threats can come from the most unlikely directions.

The Bureau of Land Management, which controls half the land in the state, rarely buys or sells land, but it does trade land in cases. In the matter at hand, BLM wanted to acquire about 1,500 acres of private land in Juab County to be added to BLM's Little Sahara Recreation Area. In exchange BLM offered public lands in trade to the private landowner.

Controversy arose when the private landowner selected various public tracts which he thought would be advantageous in one way or another. Several of his initial selections eventually were withdrawn by BLM on different grounds.

The most controversial tract surrounds a highway junction immediately east of Torrey. Containing 235 acres, it consists of a high bench and almost a mile of highway frontage, commanding spectacular views of Thousand Lake Mountain and the skyline of Capitol Reef National Park.

Gloria and I joined others in protesting the trade on several grounds. We argued that BLM's trade appraisal of the tract was too low. Of even greater importance to us personally was the tract's exceptionally strategic location. In our opinion it was a crucial element in preserving the integrity of the park's environs, and we asked that BLM retain some if not all of the tract for public use.

BLM did hold a public meeting, received comments, and made an environmental study of sorts. After a full year's consideration, however, BLM had not announced a decision or even given a hint as to what that decision was likely to be.

Environmental opponents invited the National Parks and Conservation Association to intercede. Eventually, being unsure of what BLM would do and wanting to find a reasonable solution, NPCA obtained the mediating assistance of the Trust for Public Lands. They met with the private landowner and worked out an agreement whereby most of the scenic highway frontage would forever remain undeveloped (inviolate). Also, the landowner agreed to certain other covenants. On the basis of that agreement, BLM finally transferred the land to private ownership.

Despite a fairly reasonable resolution of this affair, it is our opinion that BLM did not honor its public trust, inasmuch as it showed so little concern for scenic and public use values of the Torrey Tract, particularly when those were so outstanding and the tract was so close to a national park.

On the evidence, it seems that BLM would have allowed development of any kind to take place on that tract without restriction. It rejected every point of objection raised by opponents. It refused to make a reappraisal, despite inconsistencies and other defects in its appraisal. It wanted no direct involvement in the compromise arranged between the private landholder and the NPCA.

Such a "stand-tough" attitude, if not modified, does not bode well for the environmental future of the Plateau when BLM lands are involved - and BLM lands comprise the largest ownership parcel on the Plateau.

Furthermore, the entire congressional delegation of Utah, to our knowledge, were in favor of the Torrey trade, as originally proposed, on the "Sagebrush Rebellion" premise that public land should pass to private ownership whenever possible.

. . . . The omens I have described certainly do not encourage optimism as to the intelligent, enlightened development of the Plateau. They indicate the probability that development will proceed along the age-old track of laissez faire enterprise: unrestrained special interests devoted to the attainment of immediate or short-range, narrow, selfish goals.

There is exaggeration here, of course. Selfish interests are restrained somewhat by law, regulation and opinion - all of which, unfortunately, can be circumvented or manipulated in cases and therefore are not always dependable defenses.

In the Enchanted Wilderness Bulletin (No. 3), I described a potential future for the Plateau that could be termed "frightful". That article was written in 1971. Was it prophetic? Not entirely, I am pleased to say. To a definite extent, however, it has proved prophetic, and it promises to be even more prophetic within the foreseeable future:

We see things happening and being planned for this region that are, in our opinion, frightful. We see development money flowing in great volume toward this "economic colony", following the age-old pattern of exploitation-now and the future be damned. (Dinosaur-thinking, we call it.)

We see scores of government agencies (who control most of the Plateau) planning for, disposing of, and otherwise determining the ultimate fate of this match-less land, plunging ahead with their individual programs without adequate knowledge of what is being done by other agencies, individuals or business firms.

We see countless hungry eyes, surrounding our Enchanted Wilderness, sizing up its wealth, appraising the multiple opportunities for exploitation. . . .

We see environment-oriented groups, all of them operating on financial shoestrings with little more than dreams and idealism to buoy them up, fighting crucial battles for this or that isolated cause. Their efforts may have incalculable results, but we fear that their immediate objectives are too limited to save the region as a whole.

We see the inner region's few thousand residents trying to decide what is most important: the "progress" of economic development and population growth to bolster

their sagging economic base, or the virginity of the
land they love in their diverse ways. . . .

And finally - off in the far-away distance (but perhaps not so far after all) - we see a sad vision of the
former Enchanted Wilderness, no longer deserving of
such a name. In our vision it has become a combination
amusement and industrial park. Paved highways spider-
web the land. Rural valleys and mountain slopes are
dotted with campgrounds, trailer villages and summer
homes. Skies are marred by jet trails, industrial
plumes and smog. The erstwhile primeval silence is
shattered by the roar of planes, helicopters, cycles,
boats, mining machines, power plants, trucks, cars
and noisy voices. Public recreation parks are adjoined
by gaudy commercial and industrial developments,
including unsightly mines, and monster signs obscure
the view in every direction.

Quaint and rustic pioneer settlements have changed
into ugly communities of the modern age. The few
remaining miles of free-flowing rivers carry a torrent
of boats and boaters, who overwhelm the limited camp-
sites and create a major sanitation problem. National
forests are overrun with lumbering crews, campers,
hikers, picnickers, riders and trail bikers.

Dams and man-made lakes are scattered across the
landscape, surrounded by roads, parking lots, ramps,
camp and picnic areas, toilets, trailers, tents, cabins
and denuded shorelines. Even the red-rock wilderness
is no longer wild: its silence has long ago disappeared;
its remoteness is only a memory; its special magic,
never appreciated by those in power and of no utili-
tarian value, has evaporated before the wind of "progress".

Mining dumps and plants, giant solar evaporation
and tailings ponds, vast shale and coal strip mines,
oil and gas pumps and pipelines, enormous power generation plants and thousands of miles of power lines -
all of these and more have long since mutilated the
unique landscape that was given to mankind as a special
heritage and violated with little more forethought,
vision and concern than it has always exercised in con-
quering the earth.

I exaggerate, of course, but not as much as critics
will claim. Everything listed in this vision is already
true to some extent, and every day brings the vision
closer to ultimate fulfillment. Insofar as the Colo-

rado Plateau is concerned, mankind seems to have learned little in developing new lands except for some changes in architectural styles and industrial techniques.

Esthetics? What's that? Coordinated Planning and Zoning? Too much bother - too many obstacles - impossible! Besides, who wants to give up any of his authority?

Why worry? Sometimes we wonder. . . . After all, Big Brother controls most of this land, and doesn't he have superior vision and idealism? Won't he watch out for our best interests and those of our descendants? And where Big Brother is derelict, won't the environmental watchdog groups protect us?

. . . I am positive in my own mind about two things, (1) that unless a cooperative approach to regional planning and zoning is taken in the near future, and (2) unless the world at large becomes acquainted with this matchless land and what is happening to it, the Enchanted Wilderness as we know it - and as it conceivably could remain to some extent - is doomed to certain extinction.

## DIRECTIONS

*We love the Colorado Plateau country and we are convinced that if there indeed exists any genuinely holy place on Earth, that place is not in Mecca, not in Jerusalem, not in Rome, not in any such place. More likely (and I mean this in all seriousness) it is located somewhere within a few hundred miles of the Utah-Arizona border.*

Dr. L. Lasky, Queens, New York

With respect to the future of the Colorado Plateau, I believe the most encouraging trend of all is increased public awareness of the unique scenic, recreational and esthetic values of the Plateau. Today, millions of people come to the region just to see its marvels; and they come not only from states of the nation but from other countries as well.

How many books and articles have been written since 1971, singing the Plateau's praises? How many millions of dollars have been spent in advertising its attributes?

Widespread awareness is crucial for the region's ultimate salvation. So, too, are the efforts of individuals and groups who see the vision of its sanctity.

Back in 1971 environmentalists concentrated their meager resources primarily in battling the power plant threat and new highways through the Escalante-Glen Canyon wilderness. The tactic then (a necessity since environmental forces were few and adversaries many) was to focus on individual skirmishes. There was not the extent of concern for the region that exists now. Environmentalists are greater in number and influence today; if still deficient, these factors do have impact.

Visionary activists, fortunately, have the support of thousands of well-wishers, who are willing to contribute money and write letters. Together they can and do influence officials and lawmakers. Sometimes this influence is sufficient to preserve the rare and precious.

Among the joyful occasions of my life and Gloria's have been those times when we meet, or talk with on the phone, or trade letters with kindred enthusiasts who share our love for this country. The joy is even greater if we find that they share our vision of its "ought-to-be" regional destiny.

To us, just loving the region with passion qualifies a person for admittance to a special sanctum: a Memorial Hall of the Environment. If that person also happens to be an activist on behalf of preserving the region's natural integrity, then we bestow our personal blessings.

Among those who deserve recognition and honor for directing public attention to the landscape, its promise, worth, problems and perils are writers such as Edward Abbey, photographers such as Eliot Porter, leaders and activist members in the Sierra Club, The Wilderness Society, National Parks and Conservation Association, Utah Wilderness Association, Southern Utah Wilderness Alliance, Escalante Wilderness Committee, Friends of the Earth, Earth First!, Utah Nature Society, and similar groups in the adjoining Four Corners states.

Political leaders and government officials exercise great influence on the Plateau's fate, for good or bad, better or worse. Decisions by the uninspired can wreak havoc.

Conversely, if government people recognize the region's worth and potential, their actions can result in incalculable benefit. Take, for example, two secretaries of the Interior, Stewart Udall and Cecil Andrus. Udall fell in love with Canyonlands (being a native of Arizona, that was understandable), and he was instrumental in creating Canyonlands National Park, expanding Arches and Capitol Reef national monuments, and upgrading those monuments to national park status. Senator Frank Moss worked with Udall in those achievements. Other government figures could be mentioned in this vein.

Andrus is an environmental hero because he refused to allow construction of the proposed Intermountain Power Project in a fantastically beautiful wild area near Cathedral Valley (Capitol Reef National Park). That project, incidentally, would have been as gross an environmental affront as the nuclear waste dump near Canyonlands National Park.

In negative contrast to Udall and Andrus, in these instances, it must be observed that officials and politicians have been responsible for Glen Canyon Dam and Lake Powell ... for proposals to dam the Colorado River in Grand Canyon and the Yampa River in Dinosaur National Monument ... for the near-inundation of Rainbow Bridge ... for proposals to hasten the transfer of public lands to private ownership ... for opposition to wilderness establishment and enlargement of national parks ... for indefinite continuation of grazing in national parks ... for supporting (or not opposing) industrialization adjoining national parks and in national recreation areas ... for proposals to pave roads in parks and wild lands ... and so on down a list of travesties, proposed or executed.

Many environmental activists are driven by passion and indignation. Witness this comment by one of them: "The whole Glen Canyon dam and recreation area is the greatest monument to man's greed since time began." Not all, perhaps, would state the case quite so strongly.

What do environmentalists want? (Some prefer to be known as conservationists.) Perhaps their preferences and causes are as diversified as the individuals. They do, however, tend to agree on certain key points such as the following:

... Wilderness is vital to the human spirit, especially in this age of urban/industrial/technological stress and confinement.

... Designated wilderness areas amount to only a small part of total land in the nation. Proposed BLM wilderness in Utah's part of the Plateau is less than half that desired by wilderness supporters.

... Developmental pressures against wild and undeveloped lands are becoming more severe.

Valley of the Gods and Comb Ridge from Cedar Mesa (above).

Factory Butte on Factory Bench.

... Those who like to hike and enjoy unspoiled nature believe they have a <u>right</u> to preserve a portion of the public domain as wilderness - as much right, for instance, as other interested groups claim on behalf of development.

... At the very least, when development or conversion of wild areas are proposed, the public has a right to be fully informed and to participate in decision making.

... Future generations deserve, will need, and will want wilderness. They are likely, also, to demand, need and appreciate leisure experiences in nature to a greater extent than past or present generations.

... Wilderness lost today can never be regained.

... It is shortsightedness, even dereliction, to exhaust nature's bounty for the sake of present expediency, without due regard to husbanding for the future.

Environmental activists have a real advantage which they don't always seize. That is, they represent almost a religious cause that enables them to appeal for support and sympathy on the basis of emotion. Right versus wrong. Beauty versus ugliness. Sanctity versus desecration. Wildness versus indiscriminate change. Unselfishness versus greed. Future needs versus present self-serving. Over and over, history repeats itself with illustrations of how emotional zeal and conviction can successfully challenge political or economic expediency.

This is not to claim that every environmental cause is eminently justifiable or even reasonable. Certainly the issues listed in the paragraph above are not as clear-cut as they are written. Environmentalists are not always the knights in white, battling the forces of darkness. Or certainly their opponents do not consider them so. Adversaries often consider them abrasive, unreasonable, demanding, radical, even rabid in cases.

If there must be an adversarial relationship, however - as there so often is in controversy - which is the most advantageous public image to have: good or bad, white or black? Knowing that only rarely will they ever get what they ask (compromise is the usual order of the day), environmentalists are forced by circumstance to demand more than they expect to get. And - as with all pilgrims - environmental activists often endure abuse and disapproval.

It is a tragedy that there is such a paucity of political leaders who have a vision of the spiritual-recreational-esthetic potential of the Plateau that corresponds to the vision of activist environmentalists.

This paucity is more marked <u>within the state</u> than without, a ratio that supports the proposition that <u>Utahns don't appreciate their red-rock country as they should, don't deserve it, and therefore have forfeited whatever rights of priority they might otherwise have claimed.</u>

**Charged with its husbanding, they have failed the charge.**

Environmental laws and regulations, both federal and state, have been placed on the books since our little organization was active. They are valuable weapons in the battle for the Plateau. In particular, those federal laws and regulations, designed for the good of the nation, are a godsend to the cause of opposing traditional runaway development in the Plateau. Though not infallible safeguards, they do encourage more reasoned and open decision making.

How should controversial development in the Plateau be decided?

More often than not, decisions to date have been made on a case by case basis, after sometimes bitter confrontation, public wrangling, the flexing of muscle, political maneuvering, etc. Rarely do local decisions involve or consider more than local interests. Even less often do they consider effects on a widespread region.

Is this democracy-in-action occurring on an enlightened level? Is it the best we can or should expect? Is "case-by-case" the most reasonable, intelligent, productive way to settle disputes?

I think not. Surely it is not the way to preserve the unique attributes of the Plateau for our lifetime and the future. Systematic regional planning would be ideal, as described in Part Five. Even a degree of coordination between development interests would be superior to the individualistic anarchy prevailing today.

Unfortunately, few environmentalists, let alone politicians and government officials, see the New World vision or the Millennial Dream - or at least they consider them pie-in-the-sky fantasies.

Whether or not coordinated planning becomes a reality, we support this premise:

*Controlled travel and recreation (including esthetic enjoy-*

*ment) are the highest uses to which much of the Enchanted
Wilderness should be devoted - not always to the exclusion
of other uses, but certainly to the degree of making those
"highest uses" the common denominator for measuring desirability of other uses.*

That premise does not seem too far removed from what is
already accepted by some political leaders, officials, members of the public, and environmentalists. If some of
these people do not think of Plateau development in exactly
those terms, probably they would not be too averse to considering the premise as a common ground for discussion.

Our premise does define a standard, or common denominator, with which proposed developments can be evaluated.
By itself it will never settle controversy in specific
instances. Required for that is discussion in good faith
between interested parties. Informed public participation
on a meaningful scale also is a requirement.

**Absolutely necessary, above all other factors, is the
realization (however vague) that here in the Colorado
Plateau is a most distinctive part of the world.**

Whether the Plateau's ineffable attributes are recognized today – whether they are appreciated now or not –
some day an unmutilated Enchanted Wilderness could offer
esthetic-spiritual sanctuary to people from all parts of
the world. Present trends and future likelihoods should
be prime considerations in all discussions of changing
the natural status of the region.

Even today the Plateau's esthetic-spiritual-recreational
attributes are appreciated by thousands of pilgrims, flee-
ing from urban oppression, seeking solace-release-meaning-
natural roots-whatever. What is the situation likely to
be even a few years from now?

*The Enchanted Wilderness concept touches every
aspect of our life today: Our culture, our social and
ecological problems. Such problems, of course, are
world wide. But, in the western United States, a
region teeters on the brink of ecological disaster - a
land, paradoxically, that lies waiting to spark a
movement. That movement, once and for all, could turn
America's awareness to higher values: to preservation,
to caring, to understanding of wilderness and its role
as a psychological, emotional necessity for people
locked into urban living, longing for a place where
they can touch some semblance of their real being.*

Gloria